熟语大大学

Learn Chinese The Fun Way

汪惠迪　辑

李成业
　　　　译
郑民威

梁锦泉
黄志强　插图
林德生

联邦出版社·联合早报

© 1995联邦出版(新)私人有限公司
A member of the Times Publishing Group
Times Centre
1 New Industrial Road
Singapore 1953

1995年初版

ISBN 981 01 3061 9

Printed by Mentor Printers Pte Ltd, Singapore

目　录

成语

1 ● 按兵不动

2 ● 安份守己

3 ● 安营扎寨

4 ● 班门弄斧

5 ● 悲欢离合

6 ● 避重就轻

7 ● 变本加厉

8 ● 别出心裁

9 ● 彬彬有礼

10 ● 不言而喻

11 ● 藏龙卧虎

12 ● 趁火打劫

13 ● 处心积虑

14 ● 川流不息

15 ● 大惊失色

16 ● 大惊小怪

17 ● 德高望重

18 ● 低声下气

19 ● 颠扑不破

20 ● 东奔西跑

21 ● 独占鳌头

22 • 分身乏术

23 • 凤毛麟角

24 • 夫唱妇随

25 • 负荆请罪

26 • 敷衍塞责

27 • 根深蒂固

28 • 孤家寡人

29 • 孤苦零丁

30 • 光天化日

31 • 滚瓜烂熟

32 • 过五关，斩六将

33 • 海底捞针

34 • 含沙射影

35 • 后顾之忧

36 • 后来居上

37 • 化险为夷

38 • 见仁见智

39 • 接二连三

40 • 津津乐道

41 • 紧锣密鼓

42 • 井井有条

43 • 旧雨新知

44 • 举世闻名

45 • 口碑载道

46 • 快马加鞭

47 ● 狼吞虎咽

48 ● 力不从心

49 ● 礼轻情义重

50 ● 两败俱伤

51 ● 炉火纯青

52 ● 落落大方

53 ● 妙语如珠

54 ● 莫衷一是

55 ● 牛刀小试

56 ● 弄巧反拙

57 ● 攀龙附凤

58 ● 前事不忘，后事之师

59 ● 倾家荡产

60 ● 罄竹难书

61 ● 求才若渴

62 ● 任劳任怨

63 ● 如梦初醒

64 ● 塞翁失马，焉知非福

65 ● 三长两短

66 ● 神魂颠倒

67 ● 神通广大

68 ● 十恶不赦

69 ● 事半功倍

70 ● 事与愿违

71 ● 拭目以待

72 ● 恃强凌弱

73 ● 数一数二

74 ● 束手无策

75 ● 四面楚歌

76 ● 堂堂正正

77 ● 讨价还价

78 ● 天方夜谭

79 ● 天伦之乐

80 ● 天罗地网

81 ● 挺身而出

82 ● 同舟共济

83 ● 推三阻四

84 ● 拖泥带水

85 ● 挖空心思

86 ● 万变不离其宗

87 ● 忘年之交

88 ● 威风凛凛

89 ● 为人师表

90 ● 为所欲为

91 ● 无懈可击

92 ● 心花怒放

93 ● 兴风作浪

94 ● 形形色色

95 ● 休戚相关

96 ● 炎黄子孙

97 ● 掩人耳目

98 ● 夜以继日

99 ● 一刀两断

100 ● 一望无际

101 ● 一针见血

102 ● 以儆效尤

103 ● 以身试法

104 ● 用心良苦

105 ● 有目共睹

106 ● 怨天尤人

107 ● 乍暖还寒

108 ● 重赏之下，必有勇夫

109 ● 忠心耿耿

110 ● 自食其力

111 ● 自投罗网

俗语

112 ● 八九不离十

113 ● 病急乱投医

114 ● 长痛不如短痛

115 ● 大丈夫能屈能伸

116 ● 儿孙自有儿孙福，莫为儿孙作牛马

117 ● 好了伤疤忘了疼

118 ● 女大十八变

119 • 人一走，茶就凉

120 • 杀鸡何须用牛刀

121 • 跳到黄河洗不清

122 • 一个巴掌拍不响

慣用语

123 • 财神爷

124 • 吃回头草

125 • 传声筒

126 • 打头阵

127 • 代罪羊

128 • 兜圈子

129 • 放一马

130 • 金饭碗

131 • 开倒车

132 • 卖关子

133 • 敲门砖

134 • 省油的灯

135 • 铁板一块

136 • 钻牛角尖

按兵不动　àn bīng bù dòng

　　按：控制；兵：军队；不动：不行动、不前进。原指作战时控制一部分军队暂不行动，或接到进军指示后不肯行动。现在常用来比喻（接受任务后）不肯行动。

　　例如：我问一位大学教授：中国已经进行彻底的改革，实际上也展开了全面的市场经济建设，甚至已成了"改造"社会主义计划经济体系最成功的世界典范，日本资本却对中国按兵不动，也不愿伸出援手，到底是什么原因呢？（《日本资本家仍对中国裹足不前》，1992年5月31日《联合早报》第2版）

　　"按兵"也说"按军"，"不动"也说"不举"。

To Hold An Army Back From Military Action

Originally this saying means to hold back the troops from operation in the battlefield or to refuse to act after receiving the order to advance. Now it means to refuse or be unwilling to do something one has been assigned to do.

Example: I asked a university professor why Japan has been **unwilling** to extend a helping hand to China by providing the capital China needs, in spite of the fact that China has carried out thorough market reforms and has become the most successful socialist country to transform its centrally planned economy. (Lianhe Zaobao 31/5/92)

安分守己　　ānfèn shǒu jǐ

分：本分；己：自己的活动范围。指规规矩矩不做违法的事。

例如：美国号称世界超强，还是当今世界唯一的超强，有能力挥师制裁伊拉克的胡申，派机轰炸利比亚的卡达菲，却无力保护国内各地安分守己的人民，确也是一大讽刺。（《韩裔美国人遭池鱼之殃》，1992年5月7日《联合早报》第16版）

To Abide By Society's Laws And Behave Oneself

The proverb also means to know one's place and not to ask for more than what is due to one. It is used to describe people who act responsibly and cause no trouble to others.

Example: As the only superpower today, the US wields tremendous military power and has been able to impose sanctions against Saddam Hussein and to bomb Gadaffi of Libya. Yet ironically, when it comes to protecting its own **law-abiding** citizens, it seems so inept and powerless. (Lianhe Zaobao 7/5/92)

安营扎寨　ān yíng zhā zhài

　　安、扎：安置、建立；营：营房；寨：军营四周的栅栏（zhàlan）。安置宿营地，架起帐篷，修起栅栏。指军队驻扎下来。

　　例如：数千名官兵在胜利油田的海滩上安营扎寨，支援浅海大陆架的勘探（kāntàn）开发。（《中国军队大力支援经济建设》，1992年7月25日《联合早报》第20版）

To Set Up A Camp And Establish A Stronghold

This idiom is used to describe the act of stationing an army at a certain place.

Example: A few thousand soldiers have been **stationed** on the beach off the Shengli Oil Field to support the exploration and development of the off-shore continental shelf. (Lianhe Zaobao 25/7/92)

班门弄斧　bān mén nòng fǔ

班：鲁班，中国古代的巧匠；弄斧：摆弄斧子。在鲁班门前摆弄斧子。比喻在行家（hángjia）面前显示本领。

例如：念中四的颜程伟说："第一次出国当然会紧张，尤其是到中国去，感到有点班门弄斧。不过，这是一次挑战。"（《德明中学华乐团26日起到北京上海演出》，1992年5月21日《联合早报》第7版）

To Wield An Axe On The Doorstep Of Lu Ban's House

This proverb means to show off one's inferior skills before an expert.

Example: Secondary Four student Yan Chengwei, a member of the Dunman Secondary School Chinese Orchestra which is to visit China soon, said that he was nervous because it was the orchestra's first trip abroad and because they were going to perform in China, where the orchestras are far superior. He felt as if they were going to **wield an axe on the doorstep of Lu Ban's house**. But it was a challenge too, he added. (Lianhe Zaobao 21/5/92)

悲欢离合　bēi huān lí hé

悲伤、欢乐、离别、团聚。指人生中幸和不幸的种种遭遇以及不同的心情。

例如：今年以来已有25个香港旅游团慕名前往福建省东山县"寡妇村"探寻悲欢离合的故事，海外游客已超过2,000人次。昔日（xīrì，往日、从前）"寡妇村"，今日已成旅游热点。（《福建"寡妇村"吸引游客》，1992年7月24日《联合早报》第19版）

也说"悲欢合散"或"悲欢聚散"。

The Sorrows Of Separation And The Joys Of Reunion

This idiom refers to various events in people's lives, happy and sad.

Example: Since the beginning of this year, twenty-five tour groups from Hongkong have visited the "Widows' Village" in the Dongshan District of Fujian Province to listen to stories of **the happy and sad things** that had happened there. Tourist arrivals have exceeded 2,000 to date, turning the "Widows' Village" of yesterday into a hot tourist spot today. (Lianhe Zaobao 24/7/92)

避重就轻　bì zhòng jiù qīng

避：回避；就：凑近。指承担任务时避开繁重的，只拣轻松的。也指回避要害问题，只谈次要的方面。

例如：副总理王鼎昌最近指出，政府与人民之间对政策存在着看法上的差距，他吁请基层领袖与民众多打交道，听取人民的心声。王副总理的一番话语重心长，显示政府坦然地面对难题，没有避重就轻，有助于政府今后决策过程的改善，并为加强政府与人民的联系提出一些实际的办法。（《及时觉察差距的存在》，1992年8月14日《联合早报》社论）

To Ignore The More Important Problems And Attend To The Unimportant Ones

This means to shun a difficult or important task or problem and take on an easy or unimportant one. It also means to find an easy way out of a difficulty.

Example: Deputy Prime Minister Ong Teng Cheong pointed out recently that there were differences of opinion between the government and the people concerning government policies. He appealed to grassroots leaders to mix with the people and hear their views. Mr Ong's words show that the government is willing to take the bull by the horns and does not **ignore difficult issues**. What Mr Ong suggested will help the government fine-tune its policies and strengthen its ties with the people. (Lianhe Zaobao 14/8/92)

变本加厉　biàn běn jiā lì

厉：猛烈。形容程度比原先更加深一层，或情况变得比原先更加严重。

例如：东西德统一后，东德人的失业率大增，西德人的经济负担又加重，特别是统一后的通货膨胀加剧，工资增长却反而缓慢下来，不满的情绪也就变本加厉，最后形成战后最大的一次工潮。（《德国工潮影响政治稳定》，1992年5月7日《联合早报》社论）这个例句用的是上述后一个意思。

To Aggravate A Situation

The literal translation of this idiom reads: "To change something and make the situation worse than before."

Example: Since the reunification of Germany, unemployment has risen tremendously in the east, adding on to the economic burden already borne by the people in the west, causing much dissatisfaction. **To aggravate this situation**, wages have not kept up with the rate of inflation, and this eventually resulted in the worst labour unrests since the war. (Lianhe Zaobao 7/5/92)

别出心裁　bié chū xīncái

别：另外；心裁：心里的创造和设计。独自想出一种跟大家都不一样的新主意。

例如：淡滨尼市镇会今年别出心裁，以地铁站和列车模型配合组屋构图，给该组屋区带来国庆的欢乐气息。（《各组屋区张灯结彩迎国庆，别出心裁牌坊表达爱国情怀》，1992年8月3日《联合早报》第5版）

An Original Idea Or Creation

This means an original idea or creation that is very unique and unusual.

Example: This year, the Tampines Town Council came up with another **original idea** for National Day. It built models of the MRT station, the trains, and HDB flats for display, creating a mood of joy and celebration in the estate. (Lianhe Zaobao 3/8/92)

彬彬有礼　　bīnbīn yǒu lǐ

彬彬：文雅的样子。形容人文雅而有礼貌。

例如：混乱、迷惑、失望、愤怒，这是本报记者初到巴塞罗那，对奥运组织工作留下的第一印象和感觉……还好，志愿工作人员都是年轻的大学生，个个彬彬有礼、热情大方、面带笑容，给人留下一些好印象。（《混乱、失望、愤怒 —— 奥运组织工作印象记》，1992年7月24日《联合早报》第28版）

Courteous And Gracious

The idiom is used to describe a person who is refined and courteous.

Example: When he first arrived in Barcelona, the Zaobao reporter felt bewildered, disappointed and angry at what seemed to be poor organisation and chaos at the Olympic Games. However, he was impressed with the volunteers who were helping out at the Games, most of whom were young undergraduates, as they were most **courteous and gracious** as well as warm and friendly. (Lianhe Zaobao 24/7/92)

不言而喻　bù yán ér yù

言：解释、说明；喻：明白、知道。不需要说明，就可以
了解。

例如：华文师资问题的重要性是不言而喻的。事实上，从
华文教学的长远发展来看，这几乎可以说是最重要的问题。如
果这个问题不能趁早解决，那也许在十年以后，当我们再一次
检讨华文教学时，我们可能会不知从何谈起。（《未雨绸缪解
决华文师资问题》，1992年5月12日《联合早报》社论）

也说"不言而明"。

It Is Understood Without Saying

This idiom has an English equivalent: "It goes without saying".
It means obvious or self-evident.

Example: The importance of qualified teachers is **obvious**. It is,
in fact, the most important issue in the long run for the teaching and
learning of Chinese Language. If we do not look into this problem
now, we would produce no result even after ten years from now when
we will have the next review on the teaching of Chinese Language.
(Lianhe Zaobao 12/5/92)

藏龙卧虎 *cáng lóng wò hǔ*

比喻潜藏着各种人才。

例如：在纽约，你只要打几个电话，隔天就可以有50位电影剪辑师等着让你面试，演员就更不用说了……纽约藏龙卧虎，人才都集中在这里。（《东西文化交流可以通过电影》，1992年5月15日《联合早报》副刊《影艺》版）

Where Dragons Hide And Tigers Crouch

This idiom describes a place where one can find all sorts of talents.

Example: In New York, all you need to do is to make a few telephone calls and you will have fifty film editors turning up for an interview the next day. You will have even more actors turning up if you just request for one. New York is a place **where dragons hide and tigers crouch**: you find all kinds of talents here. (Lianhe Zaobao 15/5/92)

趁火打劫　chèn huǒ dǎjié

趁：利用机会。趁人家失火的时候去抢人家的东西。比喻趁别人危难的时候去捞好处。

例如：一名曾赢得300万美元（489万新元）加利福尼亚大彩奖金的男子，星期二被控上法庭，罪名是在上个月发生的洛杉矶暴乱事件期间趁火打劫，家中藏了一批电视机和电子仪器。（《曾赢489万元大奖男子，趁洛城暴乱抢劫财物》，1992年5月28日《联合早报》第29版）

"打劫"也说"抢劫"。

To Loot During A Fire

This proverb means to profit by others' misfortune.

Example: A man who won US$3,000,000 (S$4,890,000) in the California lottery was charged in court on Tuesday for **looting during the Los Angeles riots** last month. Some allegedly stolen television sets and electronic appliances were found in his house. (Lianhe Zaobao 28/5/92)

处心积虑　chǔ xīn jī lǜ

处心：存心；积虑：早就有了某种打算。指早已想尽一切办法盘算（含贬义）。

例如：美国的有关官员说，这个贩毒集团处心积虑，不惜工本，花了220万美元买下三家运输公司、一家巴士旅游公司、存货场和一家旧车行，装成做正经生意。（《美肃毒立大功，破获27亿元毒品》，1992年8月6日《联合早报》封面版）

To Deliberate On A Plan For A Long Time

This means to plan far ahead and find ways and means to do something, usually something bad or wrong.

Example: According to the American official, the syndicate had tried to **find ways and means** to put up a facade of doing legitimate business. It bought three companies, one a tourist coach company, another a stockyard, and the third a second-hand car company, at a great cost of US$2,200,000 for that purpose. (Lianhe Zaobao 6/8/92)

川流不息　chuān liú bù xī

川：河流；息：停止。像河水那样流个不停。比喻来往的人或车辆、船只很多。

例如：大家互相祝贺，在川流不息的人群当中，我的心平静而新奇。在我不短的电影生涯中，我从没有参加过开镜仪式。对这次开拍仪式，我感到特别新奇。（《我拍〈风华绝代〉》，1992年5月29日《联合早报》副刊《小说》版）

Flowing Endlessly Like A Stream

This saying is used to describe a heavy human, vehicular or sea traffic.

Example. In the crowd which **flowed endlessly like a stream**, I saw people congratulating one another. I remained calm but could not help being curious. In my long movie career, I had not attended any inaugural ceremony of a film production before. (Lianhe Zaobao 29/5/92)

大惊失色　dà jīng shī sè

大吃一惊，脸色都变了。形容非常吃惊。

例如：中国跳水队总教练徐益明说，伏明霞拿这面金牌是应该的，她的水平比其他选手显然高出一级。伏明霞的教练于芬补充说：“我认为伏明霞只发挥出80%的水平。”外国记者们听了，大惊失色。（《奥运史上最年轻跳水皇后，伏明霞翻腾摘桂冠》，1992年7月29日《联合早报》第28版）

A Big Fright Causes The Face To Lose Its Colour

This means taking people by surprise.

Example: Xu Yiming, the chief coach of the Chinese Diving Team, said that Fu Mingxia deserved the gold medal. Her standard was obviously much higher than those of other competitors. Fu's coach, Yu Fen, added, "I think she has only shown 80% of what she is capable of." When foreign journalists heard this, **the big fright caused their faces to lose colour**. (Lianhe Zaobao 29/7/92)

大惊小怪   *dà jīng xiǎo guài*

形容对不值得奇怪的事，表现出过分的惊奇。

例如：四年前，当他们开始比较亲密地来往时，碧云却有点怕让朋友知道。但是，朋友的反应却出乎她意料之外，没有人大惊小怪，也没有人嘲笑她，有的只是真诚的祝福。（《社交发展署会员不怕"爆光"，缘来共舞迎国庆》，1992年8月3日《联合早报》第3版）

Have A Great Fright Over Something Unimportant

This idiom means to be greatly surprised about something which should not be surprising at all or to make a fuss over something trivial.

Example: Four years ago, when they first began to go steady, Biyun was afraid of letting her friends know about her boyfriend. When her friends finally found out, their reaction was not what she had expected. None of them **made a fuss** over it. None of them laughed at her. All they did was to shower her with their blessings. (Lianhe Zaobao 3/8/92)

德高望重 *dé gāo wàng zhòng*

德：品德；高：崇高；望：声望。品德高尚，声望很高。常用来称颂年龄大而有名望的人。

例如：在薄一波主持的中顾委常委、委员茶话会上，与会者大多表示，中国全国政协主席一职历来都由德高望重者出任，虽然具体工作不一定由他去做。（《谁将问鼎中国下届政协主席？》，1992年8月10日《联合早报》第15版）

"德高"也说"德隆"（隆：高）、"德尊"（尊：高）或"德深"（深：深厚）。

High Virtue And Good Reputation

This idiom is used to describe an old and respectable person.

Example: At the tea-party dialogue session conducted by Bo Yibo, most of the participants indicated that the post of the chairman of the Political Consultative Conference was all along held by a person of **high virtue and good reputation**, even though he might not have to do any work in actual fact. (Lianhe Zaobao 10/8/92)

低声下气　dī shēng xià qì

形容恭敬顺从，不敢大声说话的样子。

　　例如：俄罗斯人民对他（指耶尔辛）这一番形同出卖国家尊严（zūnyán），低声下气的话（指耶尔辛在美国国会发表的演说）有何反应，还有待观察。（《大丈夫能屈能伸》，1992年6月21日《联合早报》第2版）

To Speak In A Soft Voice And With A Low Breath

This means to be respectful and subservient.

Example: Yeltsin's address to the U.S. Congress amounts to a selling out of Russia's national pride. What sort of reaction the Russian people will have to his speech, **spoken in a soft voice and with a low breath**, remains to be seen. (Lianhe Zaobao 21/6/92)

颠扑不破　diān pū bù pò

颠：跌；扑：敲。不管怎样摔打都不破，比喻言论或学说永远不能被推翻。

例如：韩国羽总秘书朴（piáo）忠桂在不久前曾透露，只要夺得奥运金牌，韩国球员将能终身获得每月1000美元的奖励。

"重赏之下，必有勇夫"，这真是颠扑不破的真理。（《印尼金牌奖金可能达80万元》，1992年8月6日《联合早报》第27版）

Unbreakable Even When Dropped Or Hit

This means irrefutable. The idiom is used to describe a theory or statement which always holds true.

Example: The secretary of the Korean Badminton Federation disclosed not long ago that if they could win a gold medal in the Olympic Games, Korean players would each get US$1,000 per month for life as a reward.

"A handsome reward will draw a brave man." This is indeed **a statement that will always hold true**. (Lianhe Zaobao 6/8/92)

东奔西跑 dōng bēn xī pǎo

朝东边奔，向西边跑。形容到处奔走或为某一目的而四处活动。多指为生活而到处奔走。

例如：郭进财说："新加坡要发展华乐是很困难的，从一些在本地搞华乐的朋友口中知道，他们为了生活时常得东奔西跑。"（《狮城唢呐宝岛吹响》，1992年7月28日《联合早报》副刊《少男少女》版）

也说"东奔西走"或"东奔西波"。

To Rush East And Run West

This idiom is used to describe the act of running around for a specific purpose. It usually refers to making a living.

Example: According to Guo Jincai, it is very difficult to develop Chinese music in Singapore. Those of his friends who are engaged in the promotion of Chinese music often have to **rush east and run west** in order to make a living. (Lianhe Zaobao 28/7/92)

独占鳌头 dú zhàn áo tóu

独占：独自占有或占据；鳌头：鳌是海里的大龟或大鳖（biē），鳌头是宫殿门前石阶上的巨鳌（大鳖）浮雕。科举时代进士考中状元后，要站在宫殿门前接榜，因此把中状元叫做"独占鳌头"。比喻在竞争中名列前茅。

例如：我们从近年会考成绩可以看出，几所名校独占鳌头的时代几乎可以说已成过去，好多所政府学校的成绩与自主中学比起来毫不逊色。（《让政府学校也有更多自主权》，1992年7月21日《联合早报》社论）

To Have The Head Of The Big Turtle To Oneself

During the days of the Imperial Examination system, the candidate who came in first, the "Number One Scholar", would receive his title at the big turtle sculpture in front of the palace gate. The idiom means to top the list of successful candidates.

Example: From the examination results of recent years, we can see that the days of a few well-known schools **having the head of the big turtle to themselves** are over as the performance of many government schools are as good as that of independent secondary schools. (Lianhe Zaobao 21/7/92)

分身乏术 fēnshēn fá shù

分身：抽出时间去照顾其他方面；乏：缺少；术：办法。没法抽时间去照顾别的方面。形容工作十分繁忙。

例如：在现代社会，只要是担任一两家较具规模公司的主管，就往往会觉得分身乏术，更不要说是拨出一些时间做些业务以外的事情了。（《黄思绵有三忙》，1992年7月25日《联合早报》第17版）

Unable To Split The Body

The idiom means being unable to be at two places at the same time or being too busy to spare any time for anything else.

Example: In the modern society, anyone in charge of one or two companies of some scale often feels that he is **unable to split the body**. Needless to say, he will not be able to set some time aside for anything that is not business-related. (Lianhe Zaobao 25/7/92)

凤毛麟角 fèng máo lín jiǎo

凤：凤凰；麟：麒麟。凤凰的羽毛，麒麟的角；比喻稀少。

例如：本地的英文书店以卖流行书、热门学科的入门书或参考书为主，书的品种极为普通，具有学术价值的著作更是凤毛麟角。（《浏览书店的文化气候》，1992年5月31日《联合早报》第2版）

The Phoenix's Feathers And The Unicorn's Horns

This proverb is used to describe something which is very rare or precious.

Example: The local English bookshops sell mainly popular books, beginners' handbooks or reference books on popular subjects. The range of books is quite limited. Works of academic value are few and hard to come by, as rare as **the phoenix's feathers and the unicorn's horns**. (Lianhe Zaobao 31/5/92)

夫唱妇随　fū chàng fù suí

唱：也写成"倡"，倡导。丈夫说什么，妻子跟着照办。形容夫妻相处得十分和谐。

例如：奥尔说：乔西当年"懵查查"接受他的求婚时根本不知道她会过什么样的生活，但这些年来她夫唱妇随，扮演着商人妻、州长夫人和大使夫人的角色，非常胜任愉快。（《美大使饯别会上妙语如珠，捧老婆又赞秘书》，1992年8月21日《联合早报》第12版）

The Husband Sings And The Wife Follows

This idiom is used to describe the harmonious relations between the husband and the wife.

Example: Orr said that when his wife blindly accepted his proposal to marry her long ago, she did not know at all what sort of life she would be leading. All these years, however, she has been **the wife following what the husband sings**, and has played her various roles as the wife of a businessman, governor and ambassador very well. (Lianhe Zaobao 21/8/92)

负荆请罪 fù jīng qǐngzuì

负：背着；荆：荆条，中国古代用来打人的刑具；请罪：自己犯了错误，主动请求处分。背上荆条，请对方责罚。这条成语出自《史记•廉颇蔺相如列传》，表示完全承认自己的错误，请求对方责罚和原谅。

例如：美国国会对耶尔辛的演讲报以热烈的掌声和喝采声，其实就像是对负荆请罪者给予的宽恕。（《大丈夫能屈能伸》，1992年6月21日《联合早报》第2版）

To Offer A Thorny Rod To Ask For A Flogging

The thorny rod was an instrument of torture. Offering it to ask for a flogging here means to apologise sincerely for one's mistake and ask for a pardon.

Example: The US Congress gave President Yeltsin a standing ovation for his speech. This was in fact like giving a pardon to someone who **offered a thorny rod to ask for a flogging**. (Lianhe Zaobao 21/6/92)

敷衍塞责　fūyǎn sèzé

敷衍：做事不认真，或待人不诚恳，只是表面上应付；塞责：对自己应负的责任随便应付一下，就算把事情办了。工作不认真负责，表面上应付一下。

例如：北京《人民日报》昨天报道，中共一些领导人对改革运动采取敷衍塞责的态度，有可能造成中共永远无法积极领导中国的经济建设。这家中共党报在对党内保守派进行历来最猛烈的抨击（pēngjī）时说，没有推动资本主义式经济改革的共产党人，是在危害党的利益。（《〈人民日报〉对保守派进行最猛烈抨击》，1992年7月4日《联合早报》封面版）

To Do One's Duty Perfunctorily

This idiom means to get one's work done so as to be done with it, not taking it seriously.

Example: Beijing's People's Daily reported yesterday that some Chinese Communist Party leaders had been **perfunctory in performing their duty** towards the reform movement. This could lead to a permanent setback for the Party in its efforts to reconstruct China's economy. In its strongest-ever attack on the conservatives, the paper said that communists who did not promote the capitalist-type economic reform were harming the Party's interest. (Lianhe Zaobao 4/7/92)

根深蒂固　gēn shēn dì gù

蒂：花或瓜果跟枝茎相连的部分。比喻基础牢固，不可动摇。

例如：日本若要东亚地区国家消除对它的猜疑，就应该真心诚意地对日军在第二次世界大战时的暴行表示忏悔。50年前的惨痛回忆是那样地根深蒂固，至今仍难以在东亚人民心中抹去。（《日本应争取各国信任》，1992年6月20日《联合早报》社论）

"蒂"也说"柢（dǐ，树根）。这条成语也说成"蒂固根深"或"深根固蒂"。

The Root Is Deep And The Stalk Strong

The idiom means that the foundation is strong and cannot be moved – deeply rooted in short.

Example: If Japan wants to remove the suspicion of countries in the East-Asian region, it should sincerely express repentance for the atrocities committed by the Japanese armed forces during the Second World War. The painful memories are so **deeply rooted** that they are hard to erase from the minds of East Asian people, even though it has been five decades since the war. (Lianhe Zaobao 20/6/92)

孤家寡人　　gūjiā guǎrén

孤家、寡人：都是中国古代帝王的自称。比喻孤零零的一个人，多指失掉群众、孤立而得不到别人帮助的人。

例如：瓦恩沙自从和他的革命同志 —— 团结工会的一些老搭档分手以后，他的拥护者也确实少多了。尤其是当上大总统以后，他几乎成了孤家寡人。（《瓦恩沙想做波兰的独裁者？》，1992年5月7日《联合早报》第17版）

A Person In Solitary Splendour

This idiom combines two Chinese terms both of which were used by emperors in ancient China to address themselves. Both these terms mean being all alone. The idiom can now also be used to refer to a person who is isolated because he has lost his supporters or who is simply a loner.

Example: Mr Walesa had fewer supporters after having a split with his old comrades in the Solidarity Movement. And when he was the president, he was almost like **a person in solitary splendour**. (Lianhe Zaobao 7/5/92)

孤苦零丁　gūkǔ língdīng

孤苦：很小就失去了父母；零丁：孤独，没有依靠。形容孤单困苦，无依无靠。

例如：芽笼西奖助学金及福利金委员会也拨出2000元并颁发助学金，给两名因寡母被汽车撞死而孤苦零丁的少年。（《更多一房式居民为子女申请大专助学金》，1992年5月11日《联合早报》第4版）

"零丁"也写成"伶仃"。

Being An Orphan, Lonely And Helpless

This idiomatic phrase is used at times to refer to a loner, not necessarily an orphan.

Example: The Geylang West Committee on Scholarship, Bursary and Welfare Assistance has given a grant of $2,000 on top of the bursaries it awarded to two youths who **were orphaned** when their widowed mothers were killed in road accidents. (Lianhe Zaobao 11/5/92)

光天化日　guāng tiān huà rì

光天：白天；化日：太平的日子。比喻大家都看得清清楚楚的地方。

例如：汪美珠的女儿在受访时说，虽然她母亲所住的那个地方非常偏僻，但是在光天化日下发生这种抢劫伤人案，还是第一遭。（《老妇遭劫匪毒打，脸眼肿胀身重伤》，1992年8月6日《联合早报》第3版）

In Broad Daylight

This means a place where everybody can see clearly. The expression is used to express surprise at the audacity of someone who commits a crime in the day-time, or at a public place.

Example: The daughter of Wang Meizhu said in an interview that although the place where her mother lived was quite isolated, still she was surprised that the robbery had taken place **in broad daylight**. It was the first time a robbery which caused hurt to the victim had happened. (Lianhe Zaobao 6/8/92)

滚瓜烂熟　gǔn guā lànshú

烂熟：熟透了。滚圆的瓜熟透了。形容记忆、背诵得非常
流利纯熟。

例如：在国庆日检阅礼之前，沈中校需要跟检阅队伍练习
和彩排至少40次，因此那37个口令和每个口令的程序，他都已
背得滚瓜烂熟。（《37个口令个个要清晰准确，检阅礼司令官
不易当，沈育坤家人给他打气》，1992年7月15日《联合早
报》第7版）

Thoroughly Ripe And Round Melons

This idiom means to be so familiar with something that one can
recite it very accurately and fluently.

Example: Before the National Day Parade, Lieutenant-Colonel
Shen had to train and rehearse with parade contingents at least forty
times. Thus, he had memorised the 37 commands and their sequence
like **thoroughly ripe and round melons**. (Lianhe Zaobao 15/7/92)

过五关，斩六将 guò wǔ guān, zhǎn liù jiàng

　　这条成语出自中国的章回小说《三国演义》。第27回叙述，关羽单枪匹马接连闯了东岭等五个关口，杀了六个守关的将领。比喻值得骄傲的不平凡的经历，也比喻克服重重困难。

　　例如：成为行动党候选人的过程可以用"过五关斩六将"来形容。而且获得担任支部领袖的议员推荐的人选，还必须在会见担任部长的资深党领袖时，同来自四面八方的人选互相竞争，才有望在最后一关接受以秘书长李光耀资政为首的委员会面试。（《过五关斩六将》，1992年6月20日《联合早报》第18版）

To Go Through Five Barriers And Kill Six Generals

In the famous Chinese novel, 'The Romance of the Three Kingdoms', Guan Yu went through the five mountain passes, killing the six generals guarding them. The idiom now refers to outstanding achievements or the overcoming of great difficulties.

Example: The idiom **"going through five barriers and killing six generals"** may be used to describe the process of becoming a PAP election candidate. The person selected has to compete with others during the interviews conducted by senior party leaders. It is only if he succeeds in this round that he gets to be interviewed by a committee headed by the Party Secretary-General, Senior Minister Lee Kuan Yew in the final round. (Lianhe Zaobao 20/6/92)

海底捞针　hǎi dǐ lāo zhēn

比喻很难找到或很难达到预想的目的。

例如："对付偷车贼我们还不行，"警方发言人说，"中国当局说，要在中国这么大的地方找被偷去的车，简直是海底捞针。"（《港今年上半年1776辆名贵车被偷》，1992年7月24日《联合早报》第19版）这个句子里，"海底捞针"比喻很难找到。

也说"大海捞针"／"东海捞针"／"水底捞针"。

To Fish For A Needle At The Bottom Of The Sea

This idiom means the same as "to look for a needle in a haystack" or to do an impossible or extremely difficult task.

Example: "We are not good enough yet in dealing with car thieves," the police said. "The Chinese authorities have said that to look for stolen cars in such a vast country like China is virtually like **fishing for a needle at the bottom of the sea**." (Lianhe Zaobao 24/7/92)

含沙射影　hán shā shè yǐng

　　传说水中有一种叫蜮（yù）的动物，听到人的声音，就含沙向人喷射，被射中的人，皮肤会生疮，被射中影子，也会生病。比喻暗中攻击或诽谤中伤别人。

　　例如：布斯表示，在他的竞选运动中，绝不允许人身攻击，他同时指责克林顿以含沙射影的卑劣手段说他逃税，因为他在缅因州没缴税。（《布斯不再沉默，决反攻克林顿》，1992年8月7日《联合早报》第2版）

Spitting Sand To Shoot At A Shadow

It is said that a water creature was able to spit out sand to shoot at people or their shadows when it heard any noise made by human beings. Anyone hit by the sand would fall sick. Derived from this story, the idiom means to vilify, to smear or to malign someone.

Example: Bush said that during the election campaign, he would not allow personal attacks. He also accused Clinton of resorting to **spitting sand to shoot at his shadow** by saying that he had evaded tax. (Lianhe Zaobao 7/8/92)

后顾之忧　hòu gù zhī yōu

顾：回过头来照顾；忧：忧患、忧虑。指需要回过头来照顾的令人忧虑的事情。

例如：无论是共和党的布斯总统继续执政也好，还是民主党的克林顿上台也好，只有等到中美两国在明年春季都完成政治选举之后，两国新当选（或重新当选）的领导人才能静下心来认真考虑改善中美关系的问题，而且美国方面不会再有后顾之忧。（《中美关系好像升降机》，1992年7月21日《联合早报》第30版）

"忧"也说成"患"、"虑"或"虞"（yú，忧虑）。

The Worry That Impedes One's Action

This refers to the worry or fear that stops one from going ahead with something.

Example: Whether it is Bush of the Republican Party continuing in office or Clinton of the Democratic Party going into office, it is only after the elections in China and the United States in spring next year that the newly elected (or re-elected) leaders of the two countries can seriously consider the question of improving Sino-American relations without **worries that impede their actions**. (Lianhe Zaobao 21/7/92)

后来居上　hòu lái jū shàng

原意是资格浅的人反而在资格老的人之上。现在多用来称赞后起的人或事物超过先前的。

例如：邓小平说："浦东开发是晚了，这是件坏事，但也是好事，你们可以借鉴广东的经验，可以搞得好一点，搞得现代化一点，起点高一点，后来居上，我相信这一点。"（《邓小平到上海视察》，1992年5月12日《联合早报》第15版）

The Newcomer Surpasses The Old-timer

This idiom is often used to praise a newcomer, or a newly emerging thing which is better than the existing ones.

Example: Deng Xiaoping says that the development of Putong is a little bit late. This is bad. But it is good too. The people of Putong can learn from the Guangdong experience and do it better, starting from a higher point than Guangdong and making Putong even more modern. **The newcomer surpasses the old-timer**. Deng says he always believes in this. (Lianhe Zaobao 12/5/92)

化险为夷 huà xiǎn wéi yí

险：险阻；夷：平坦、平安。原指变险阻为平坦的道路。后多用来指使危险的处境或情况变为平安。

例如：世界唯一的一名完全靠人工合成营养液孕育的女婴蔡惟，18日在上海度过她的百日生辰。在"落地"后的42天内，小蔡惟在儿科医院历经抢救，几度化险为夷。（《世界唯一靠人工营养液孕育，上海女婴安度百日》，1992年7月21日《联合早报》第21版）

To Turn Danger Into Safety

The original and literal meaning of this idiom is to turn a rough patch into a smooth track. Now it means to turn a dangerous situation into a safe one or to head off danger.

Example: Baby girl Cai Wei, the only baby in the world who fed on synthetic nutrition fluid, celebrated her 100th day in Shanghai on July 18. Within 42 days of her birth, little Cai Wei went through several rescue operations in the paediatric hospital, in which **danger was turned into safety**. (Lianhe Zaobao 21/7/92)

见仁见智　jiàn rén jiàn zhì

也说成"仁者见仁，智者见智"，意思是说对同一个问题，仁者看见它说它是仁，智者看见它说它是智。指对同一个问题，因为各人观察的角度不同，看法也就不同。

例如：假如民主党的克林顿人主白宫，中美关糸将会出现什么样的局面呢？人们对此见仁见智。（《中美关糸好像升降，1992年7月21日《联合早报》第30版）

Some Take It As Benevolent While Others Take It As Intelligent

This idiom means different people have different views or it is a matter of opinion.

Example: If, for instance, Clinton should get to the White House, what sort of situation would emerge in Sino-American relations? **Different people have different views** on this question. (Lianhe Zaobao 21/7/92)

接二连三 jiē èr lián sān

接连不断。表示同一类的事情或行动连续出现。

例如：过去牛车水的一些破旧屋宇（wū yǔ，房屋）成为一群孤苦无依的老人聚居的家，卫生设备差，也不够安全，老人死于火患的事故接二连三发生过。（《安老居计划所应考虑的问题》，1992年7月29日《联合早报》社论）

也说"叠二连三"，"叠"（dié，重复）；或"连三接四"。

To Join The Second With The Third

This describes a situation in which things of the same nature happen one after another in quick succession.

Example: In the past, the old dilapidated houses in the Kreta Ayer area were the homes of helpless old people. Sanitation facilities were as good as non-existent and the buildings were unsafe. **One fire occurred after another in quick succession**, killing many of the old people. (Lianhe Zaobao 29/7/92)

津津乐道 jīnjīn lèdào

津津：兴趣浓厚的样子；乐道：喜欢谈论。形容很有兴趣地谈论。

例如：洛杉矶种族大暴乱，除了让世人重新认识美国，重新评估美国人喜爱输出的"人权"之外，也使人对过去津津乐道的"世界各族大熔炉"又增加了一层新认识。（《韩裔美国人遭池鱼之殃》，1992年5月7日《联合早报》第16版）

To Take Delight In Talking About

The idiom means to dwell on a subject with relish.

Example: The Los Angeles riots have changed people's impression of the U.S., making them re-evaluate the U.S.'s human rights policy towards other countries. The world now sees the U.S. for what it really is, not the "great melting pot all of races" that people **take delight in talking about**. (Lianhe Zaobao 7/5/92)

紧锣密鼓　jǐn luó mì gǔ

锣、鼓：打击乐器。戏曲中，在角色出场前，常有一阵紧密的锣鼓声，为其制造气氛。锣鼓敲得很密。比喻事前紧张的准备工作。

例如：新港督彭定康正以私人名义在新加坡访问，定于9日离新赴港，正式就任香港第28任，也可能是最后一任总督。港府有关部门和各界已在紧锣密鼓，筹备迎接，届时官方和民间都会有一系列仪式和活动（《彭定康"任重道险"》，1992年7月7日《联合早报》第14版）

也说"密锣紧鼓"。

Rapid And Intense Beating Of Gongs And Drums

The idiom means the intense preparation for an important event.

Example: Mr Chris Patten, Hongkong's new governor, now on a private visit to Singapore, is due to leave Singapore for Hongkong on July 9 to officially take on his duties as Hongkong's 28th governor, possibly the last governor. The colony's government departments and the various quarters are now engaged in **rapid and intense beating of gongs and drums** to prepare a welcome for him with a series of ceremonies and activities. (Lianhe Zaobao 7/7/92)

井井有条 jǐngjǐng yǒu tiáo

井井：整齐而有秩序的样子。形容有条有理，秩序不乱。

例如：新加坡禁止香口胶，外国人觉得很可笑。虽然别人取笑我们，但新加坡毕竟是我们的家，我们把家收拾干净，井井有条，别人或许不喜欢，但这不是他们的家。（《杨荣文准将：政府不愿看到报界跟它对立》，1992年6月2日《联合早报》封面版）

"有条"也说"有方（规则）"、"有序（次序）"或"有理（条理）"。这条成语也说成"井然有序"或"井然不紊（wěn，乱）"。

To Keep In Good Order

This saying means to keep a place neat and orderly or to be very organised.

Example: When Singapore banned chewing gum, foreigners felt that it was ridiculous. But Singapore is, after all, our own country. We must **keep our house in good order**. Others may not like it, but it is not their home. (Lianhe Zaobao 2/6/92)

旧雨新知 *jiù yǔ xīn zhī*

旧雨：老朋友；新知：新结交的朋友。指新老朋友。

例如：这次到多伦多参加南洋大学全球校友联欢会，遇见了许多旧雨新知，主办当局加拿大校友全体出动，以最盛情的方式接待我们。（《从北美南大校友的成就，看传统文化的力量》，1992年7月9日《联合早报》第14版）

也说："新知旧雨"。

Old Friends And New Acquaintances

This idiom refers to long-standing friends and newly-made friends.

Example: At the Nanyang University global alumni reunion in Toronto, I met many **old friends and new acquaintances**. The alumni in Canada who organised the reunion came in full strength and gave us the warmest and grandest reception. (Lianhe Zaobao 9/7/92)

举世闻名 jǔshì wénmíng

举世：整个世界，全世界；闻名：有名。

例如：工潮少，政潮少，结果就把战后西德带上长期经济繁荣的道路，并为西德带来举世闻名的"经济奇迹"。（《德国工潮影响政治稳定》，1992年5月7日《联合早报》社论）

Of World Renown

The literal translation of this phrase reads, "Throughout the world people know the name."

Example: With fewer labour unrests and fewer political crises, Germany was able to enjoy years of uninterrupted prosperity after the war. This is an economic miracle **of world renown**. (Lianhe Zaobao 7/5/92)

口碑载道　　kǒubēi zài dào

口碑：比喻群众口头的称颂像文字刻在碑上一样。形容满路都是称颂的声音。

例如：新航不止是我国最重要的挂牌公司，在世界各大航空公司之中，它的盈利始终令人刮目相看，它的服务与管理，在国际上口碑载道，几乎成为新加坡的象征。（《新航创下另一个"新记录"》，1992年7月27日《联合早报》社论）

Verbal Monuments All Along The way

This means highly praised.

Example: The Singapore Airlines (SIA) is not only the most important listed company in Singapore, its profits, services and management make it highly esteemed amongst the world's major airline companies. SIA has **verbal monuments all along the way** internationally and this has almost made it a symbol of Singapore. (Lianhe Zaobao 27/7/92)

快马加鞭　kuài mǎ jiā biān

跑得很快的马，加上几鞭会使它跑得更快。比喻快上加快。

例如：中国领导层的智囊团曾献议，修改过去一贯反对日本大国意识的政策，而实事求是地承认它是"政治大国"。既然"政治大国"已获得北京的默许和承认，东京今后快马加鞭朝大国道路迈进，自不待言。（《再谈日本国内如何鼓吹派兵舆论》，1992年7月10日《联合早报》第15版）

To Whip A Galloping Horse More

When a horse is galloping, adding a few strokes of the whip will spur it to run faster. The idiom means to expedite or to make things move faster.

Example: The think-tank of Chinese leaders has revised its long-standing policy against Japan's "big power consciousness" and has finally recognised that Japan is a "big political power". Since that status has been tacitly endorsed by Beijing, it is needless to say that Tokyo will henceforth **whip a galloping horse more** to achieve big-power nationhood sooner. (Lianhe Zaobao 10/7/92)

狼吞虎咽 láng tūn hǔ yàn

形容吃东西又急又猛的样子；也形容大口大口地吃东西，又贪又馋（chán）的样子。

例如：在故宫博物院门口，又热又渴的中外游人簇拥（cùyōng，紧紧围着）在树荫下，围着西瓜摊狼吞虎咽，瓜皮已经堆积成山。（《北京出现十年罕见高温》，1992年7月21日《联合早报》第16版）

To Swallow Something Like Wolves And Tigers

This idiom means to gobble up or devour something ravenously.

Example: Outside the entrance of the Palace Museum, local and foreign visitors who felt hot and thirsty gathered around the water-melon stall in the shade of the tree, **swallowing water-melons like wolves and tigers**. The melon peels piled up like hills. (Lianhe Zaobao 21/7/92)

力不从心　lì bù cóng xīn

心里想做某一件事，但是力量不够。

例如：拉美地区曾经是国际资本关注的热点，目前美国与拉美地区的经济联系也十分密切，但拉美地区的大部分国家目前社会动荡不定，政治不稳，加上美国本身陷入严重的经济衰退，对许多事已经力不从心。（《机不可失，时不我待》，1992年6月5日《联合早报》第20版。时不我待：shí bù wǒ dài，成语，时间不会等待我们，指要抓紧时间。）

"心"也说"愿"（愿望）。

The Strength Does Not Meet The Heart's Desire

This means one's ability falls short of one's wish or ambition.

Example: Latin America has been a hot focal point of international capital. At the moment, the economic ties between the U.S. and the Latin American countries are very close. Most of these countries, however, are now in a state of social unrest and political instability. Itself crippled by economic recession, the U.S. finds that it is unable to do what it wishes: **its strength does not meet its heart's desire**. (Lianhe Zaobao 5/6/92)

礼轻情意重　lǐ qīng qíngyì zhòng

礼物虽然轻微，情意却很深厚。

例如：陈荣照副教授代表中文系全体教职员，赠送一副对联和一个纪念牌给林教授，中文系的同学也送了一本签名册给他留念。礼轻情意重。林徐典教授接到礼物时感动地说："这些将是我一生中永远铭记心田的最贵重的礼物。"（《回首桃李满天下，前瞻景色分外美》，1992年8月3日《联合早报》第4版）

常跟"千里送鹅毛"连着说成"千里送鹅毛，礼轻情意重"。"送"也说"寄"；"礼"也说"物"，"情"也说"人"。"千里送鹅毛"和"礼轻情意重"都可以单说；两句连着说，通常归到谚语中。

The Gift Is Light But The Goodwill Is Great

This idiom means that although the gift may be of little value, the sentiment which goes with it is great.

Example: On behalf of the staff of the Department of Chinese Studies, Associate Professor Tan Eng Chaw presented Professor Lim Chee Then (the retiring Head of Department) with a Chinese couplet and a commemorative plaque while students of the department presented him with an album. **The gift was light but the goodwill was great.** Prof Lim was moved, saying, "These are the most valuable and memorable presents I have ever received in my life." (Lianhe Zaobao 3/8/92)

两败俱伤　　liǎng bài jù shāng

俱：都、全。两方面都受到损害。

例如：泰国的情形就像我们所熟悉的人发生家变。事情闹大后，我们希望它能够及时受到控制，双方能够妥协与让步，想法子和解。只要有一方坚持到底，到头来将两败俱伤。

（《杨荣文准将：政府不愿看到报界跟它对立》，1992年6月2日《联合早报》封面版）

Both Sides Are Defeated And Wounded

It means both sides suffer in a dispute or a fight.

Example: We are concerned about what happens in Thailand, just as we are concerned about what happens to our friends . When there is a dispute, we hope that it can be resolved on time, with both sides compromising and giving in to each other, seeking ways to settle it peacefully. If one side refuses to give in, **both sides would be defeated and wounded** in the end. (Lianhe Zaobao 2/6/92)

炉火纯青　lú huǒ chún qīng

　　纯青：炉火的温度达到最高点，火焰从红色转成青色。原本指道家炼丹成功时候的火候。比喻达到纯熟完美的境界。

　　例如：共和党当局安排奎尔夫人和布斯夫人上台演讲，目的是由她们去宣扬共和党的"家庭价值"观念，也是律师的奎尔夫人所发表的演讲虽然中规中矩，但是布斯夫人的表现，则已炉火纯青。（《"夫人"对"夫人"——美国总统大选中不大不小的插曲》，1992年8月21日《联合早报》第19版）

A Stove Fire In Pure Blue Flame

When the stove fire reaches its highest temperature, its flame turns from yellow into blue. This idiom is used to describe a skill or proficiency which has reached the highest degree.

Example: The Republicans had arranged for Mrs Quayle and Mrs Barbara Bush to speak on stage to promote "family values". Although the speech given by Mrs Quayle, a lawyer, was right and proper, it was Barbara's performance which was really superb, like **a stove fire in pure blue flame**. (Lianhe Zaobao 21/8/92)

落落大方 luòluò dàfāng

落落：心胸坦率；大方：不拘束、不俗气。形容人的举止很自然，不拘谨（jūjǐn，过分地谨慎、拘束）。

例如：他们都是社交发展署的会员。当记者和摄影记者观看他们排练舞蹈时，他们在镜头前都表现得落落大方。这跟社交发展署刚开始举办活动时，参加者纷纷躲避镜头的情形相比，的确有很大的不同。（《社交发展署会员不怕"爆光"，缘来共舞迎国庆》，1992年8月3日《联合早报》第3版）

Natural and Graceful

This is used to describe the manner of being natural and at ease.
Example: They were all members of the Social Development Unit (SDU). When reporters and photographers watched them at the dance rehearsal, they all appeared very **natural and graceful** in front of the cameras. This was a far cry from the time when the SDU was first set up. At that time SDU members were very shy and avoided the cameras. (Lianhe Zaobao 3/8/92)

妙语如珠　miào yǔ rú zhū

妙语：有趣的言语；如珠：好像连接成串的珍珠。比喻有趣动听的话接连不断。

例如：台上妙语如珠，台下满堂欢笑。昨天举行的"全国中学相声表演赛"大决赛，吸引了近千名观众，大家都尽情地享受着相声这种幽默与风趣的语言艺术。（《台上相声妙语如珠，台下欢声笑语不绝》，1992年7月26日《联合早报》第14版）

Witty Words Strung Up Together Like Pearls

This idiom is used to describe witty and interesting remarks flowing freely and continuously.

Example: **Witty words strung up together like pearls** were uttered on stage while laughter burst out amongst the audience. The final round of the National Secondary School Witty Cross Talk Competition attracted an audience of nearly a thousand people. They all enjoyed this humorous and interesting art of words. (Lianhe Zaobao 26/7/92)

莫衷一是　　mò zhōng yī shì

莫：不；衷：断定；是：对、正确。不能断定哪个对，哪个不对。

例如：原北京旅游局局长薄熙成辞职一事，在海内外引起很大的反响，一时传闻很多，莫衷一是，而他本人一直回避新闻界的追踪。（《中共高干子弟的痛苦 —— 薄熙成辞官甘笑骂由人》，1992年7月29日《联合早报》第15版）

No Conclusion As To Which One Is Right

This idiom means no one can tell which is correct.

Example: The resignation of Bo Xicheng from the directorship of Beijing Tourism Bureau has stirred up many reactions both abroad and at home, giving rise to many speculations. **No one can tell which is correct**, with Bo himself avoiding the pressmen. (Lianhe Zaobao 29/7/92)

牛刀小试　niú dāo xiǎo shì

　　牛刀：宰牛用的刀；小试：稍微用一下，初步显示一下身手。比喻有大才干的人，先在小事情上稍微施展一下本领。例如：美国奥运篮球队早已到达摩纳哥进行训练。队员们多数带着家眷（jiājuàn），好像是去度假似的。对奥运会，他们心中有数。这次是趁休战期间在地中海滨度假，另一方面牛刀小试，等着拿奥运的另一面金牌。（《美国杀鸡用牛刀》，1992年7月25日《联合早报》第30版）

A Small Test Of The Big Butcher's Knife

This means a master hand showing his talent or skill in a minor or easy display.

Example: The U.S. Olympic Basketball Team had long left for training in Monaco. Most of the players brought their families along, as if they were on a holiday. They more or less knew what was going to happen at the Olympic Games. This time round they just took the opportunity to vacation at the Mediterranean beaches during the break, before they did **a small test of the big butcher's knife**. They were just waiting to score yet another gold. (Lianhe Zaobao 25/7/92)

弄巧反拙　nòng qiǎo fǎn zhuō

本想取巧，结果反而做了蠢事。

例如：纽西兰国内有一个福利计划，是特别照顾没有结婚的和离婚的妈妈的。1973年计划实行的时候，只有4000个单亲家庭，可是到今天已经增加到十万个，比住在宏茂桥和大巴窑的所有家庭还多，政府的好意却弄巧反拙，鼓励了更多人离婚和不结婚。（《人人平均的经济制度行不通》，1992年8月17日《联合早报》第10版）

也说"弄巧成拙"。

To Try To Be Clever Only To End Up Being Foolish

This refers to a deed or an action aimed at doing something better or ingeniously but which ends in a fiasco instead.

Example: In New Zealand there is a special welfare scheme that takes care of unmarried or divorced mothers. When implemented in 1973, there were only 4,000 single-parent families benefiting from the scheme, but now this figure has increased to 100,000, more than the families in Ang Mo Kio and Toa Payoh combined. The scheme was well-intentioned, but it has the undesirable result of encouraging divorces and discouraging marriage. The New Zealand government has **tried to be clever but ended up being foolish**. (Lianhe Zaobao 17/8/92)

攀龙附凤　pān lóng fù fèng

攀：双手抓住别的东西往上爬；附：依附；龙、凤：比喻有权有势的人。比喻巴结有权势的人。

例如：印尼前第一夫人蒂薇说："我的朋友和我都不喜欢她（指维多利亚·奥斯梅纳），并且对她那种企图攀龙附凤的行为感到十分厌恶。"（《两名女人积怨已久》，1992年8月14日《联合早报》第33版）

To Cling On To The Dragon And Get Close To The Phoenix

This means to rub shoulders with the powerful and the influential, in order to gain some status.

Example: The former First Lady of Indonesia said, "We absolutely abhor the way she (Victoria Osmena) **clings on to the dragon and gets close to the phoenix**. My friends and I do not like her." (Lianhe Zaobao 14/8/92)

前事不忘，后事之师　　qián shì bù wàng, hòu shì zhī shī

记住以前的经验教训，把它作为以后做事的借鉴。

例如：前事不忘，后事之师。对日本当局、日本人民和东南亚各国人民而言，记住二次世界大战的惨痛教训都是必需的。特别是日本军人再次走向东南亚的今天，这样的提醒绝不应当被视为杞人忧天。（《前事不忘，后事之师》，1992年8月6日《联合早报》社论）

A Past Event, If Not Forgotten, Is A Guide For The Future

This means that the lesson learnt in the past serves as a guide for future action.

Example: **A past event, if not forgotten, is a guide for the future**. It is necessary for the Japanese authorities, the Japanese people and the peoples of the South-east Asian countries to remember the painful experience of the Second World War. This is especially so today when the Japanese military is marching towards South-east Asia again. Such a reminder should not be dismissed as unnecessary. (Lianhe Zaobao 6/8/92)

倾家荡产　qīng jiā dàng chǎn

倾：倒出；荡：搞光。家产全部丧失。

例如：绝大部分股民认为只要买股票，就能发财，没有人相信股市具有极大的风险，随时可能叫人倾家荡产。（《从深圳股市风潮看中国股市问题》，1992年8月12日《联合早报》第14版）

"荡产"也说"尽产"、"破产"或"竭产"（竭：jié，尽）。

To Empty The Home And Clear Out The Properties

This idiom describes losing everything one has.

Example: Most of the share punters think that they can make money by buying shares. They do not seem to believe that there are risks involved in the share market which can **empty their homes and clear out their properties**. (Lianhe Zaobao 12/8/92)

罄竹难书 qìng zhú nán shū

罄：尽；竹：做竹简的竹子，竹简是古代用来写字的竹片。指事实很多，写不完。现在多用来形容罪状多得写不完，含有贬义。

例如：中国作为一个受害国，在任何时候都有权利批评谴责日本当年的侵略行为，日本军队对中国老百姓所犯下的罪行，更是伤天害理，罄竹难书。（《日皇到底访不访华》，1992年7月14日《联合早报》社论）

Impossible To Record Even By Using Up All The Bamboo Strips

Bamboo strips were used for writing in ancient China. This idiom means that the incidents, crimes or atrocities are too many or numerous to record.

Example: As a victim country, China has the right to criticise and condemn Japan for its invasion in the past. The atrocities committed by the Japanese armed forces against the common people of China were acts which hurt heaven and harmed principles. Such acts were **impossible to record even by using up all the bamboo strips**. (Lianhe Zaobao 14/7/92)

求才若渴　qiú cái ruò kě

求：寻求；才：有才能的人；若渴：好像口干想喝水一样。形容迫切地寻求人才。

例如：高科技工商时代，求才若渴，一些先进国家纷纷采取优惠政策，吸引外来人才，国与国之间体制不一，加上贫富不均，更直接地刺激了移民浪潮。（《把人才外流化为有利因素》，1992年7月29日《联合早报》第14版）

To Seek Talents Like Thirst Seeking Water

This idiom refers to the urgent need to look for talents.

Example: In the age of high-tech industry and commerce, **seeking talents is like thirst seeking water**. Advanced countries vie with one another to offer favourable terms to attract foreign talents. The different political systems in the countries, coupled with the imbalance between the rich countries and the poor countries, have directly stimulated the waves of migration. (Lianhe Zaobao 29/7/92)

任劳任怨　rèn láo rèn yuàn

任：担当；劳：劳苦；怨：别人对自己的埋怨。形容做事不怕辛苦，不怕招人埋怨。

例如：改变教学要真正有成效，华文教师的积极态度还是比什么都重要。我们应该改善华文教师的地位，提高他们的士气，但我们也期待华文教师继续发挥任劳任怨的精神。（《改进华文教学的三项因素》，1992年5月11日《联合早报》社论）

To Work Hard And Put Up With Criticism

The idiom also means to willingly bear the burden of office.

Example: There is nothing more important than the positive attitude of the Chinese Language teachers. To improve the teaching and learning of the language, we should improve their morale by raising their status. But we must expect them to continue to uphold the spirit of **working hard and putting up with criticism**. (Lianhe Zaobao 11/5/92)

如梦初醒 rú mèng chū xǐng

好像做梦刚醒。比喻从胡涂、错误的认识中刚刚醒悟过来。

例如：从1986年夺得世界杯后，美国队就接连败给巴西、苏联和南斯拉夫，失去了世界杯霸主的地位，也丢了奥运会的金牌，并在泛美运动会（两次）和世界友好运动会失杯，其中三次还只得铜牌（奥运、泛美和世界杯各一次），这才如梦初醒，觉得他们的王国受到了严重的威胁和挑战，不得不另谋良策。（《美国杀鸡用牛刀》，1992年7月25日《联合早报》第30版）

Just Like Waking Up From a Dream

This idiom means to become enlightened suddenly or to realise something suddenly.

Example: Since losing the World Cup in 1986 the American team was defeated successively by Brazil, Russia and Yugoslavia, losing the World Cup championship and the Olympic Gold. But it was only after the Americans lost the championship in the Pan-American Games and the World's Friendship Games, winning only a bronze on three occasions, that they **woke up from their dream** to realise that their supremacy was seriously threatened and challenged and that they had to do something about it. (Lianhe Zaobao 25/7/92)

塞翁失马，焉知非福 sài wēng shī mǎ, yān zhī fēi fú

塞：边界上的险要地方；翁：老头儿；焉：哪里、怎么（常用来表示反问）。住在边塞（biānsài）上的老头儿丢了一匹马，别人安慰他，他却说："怎么知道这不是福呢？"几个月后，这匹马果然带了一匹好马回来。比喻暂时受了损失，却因此得到好处；也指坏事可以变成好事。

例如：我们当然要防止人才外流，促使回流。但是，如果把眼光放远，人才外流并不是绝对的弊端（bìduān，损害公益的事情），有道是塞翁失马，焉知非福。（《把人才外流化为有利因素》，1992年7月29日《联合早报》第14版）

"焉知"也说"安知"，"安"跟"焉"意思相同。

When The Old Frontier Man Lost His Horse, Who Knew Whether It Was Fortunate Or Not?

The old man living at the frontier lost his horse. When others comforted him, he said, "Who knows? This may be a good thing." After a few months, the horse which he had lost came back with a fine stallion. The idiom means that a misfortune can turn out to be a good thing.

Example: We should, of course, prevent a brain-drain and promote the return of talents. If we look far ahead, a brain-drain is not an absolute evil. As the saying goes, **"When the old frontier man lost his horse, who knew whether it was fortunate or not?"** (Lianhe Zaobao 29/7/92)

三长两短 sān cháng liǎng duǎn

指意外的灾祸或事故。常用作"死亡"等不幸事件的委婉语。

例如：蒋经国本来不愿到美国访问，几位秘书长也都主张不去，只有我周某主张要去，谁知发生遇刺事件。如果他真的有个三长两短，我周某的罪过可重了，在历史上我怎么交代？（《周书楷谈台湾对美外交的一段往事》，1992年8月13日《联合早报》第15版）

Three Long Two Short

This refers to an accident or a mishap and is also a euphemism for death.

Example: Chiang Ching-kuo originally did not wish to visit America and several secretaries-general also advised him against going. It was only I who advocated his visit. Who would have known that there would be an assassination attempt? If any **three long two short** should happen to him, it would be a serious mistake on my part. How would I be able to account to posterity? (Lianhe Zaobao 13/8/92)

神魂颠倒　shénhún diāndǎo

神魂：精神；神志。形容对人对事人迷到了极点，心神不定，失去常态。

例如：《每日镜报》说，在它拿到的电话录音里，查尔斯和卡米拉互诉爱恋之情，满口说"我爱你"，查尔斯还说"我为你神魂颠倒，你是我的光荣"。（《英小报拿到查尔斯谈情录音带》，1992年11月14日《联合早报》第31版）

The Soul Has Turned Upside Down

This idiom means to be so enchanted or captivated by something that one becomes clouded in the mind and acts abnormally. It is often used to describe someone who is head over heels in love.

Example: The Daily Mirror said that in the telephone tape recording it had obtained, Charles and Camilla spoke about their love for each other, with Charles saying all the time, "I love you." Charles said that he was **head over heels in love** with her and that she was his glory. (Lianhe Zaobao 14/11/92)

神通广大　shéntōng guǎngdà

神通：佛教用语，修行有成就的人具有无所不能的力量。形容本领神奇高超。

例如：一张神通广大的卡能够取代一些较次要的卡，而且目前约有三分之一年龄在12岁以上的国人，手中都有一张这样的卡。这卡就是我们的身分证。（《身有一卡，处处无"卡"》，1992年8月17日《联合早报》第5版）

Great Divine Power

This refers to infinite magical power or resourcefulness.

Example: There is one single card that is so special that it is as if it possesses **great divine power**. This card can replace some less important cards. At the moment, about one third of Singaporeans aged 12 and above already possess such cards. I am referring to the Singapore identity card. (Lianhe Zaobao 17/8/92)

十恶不赦　shí è bù shè

十恶：中国古代刑法所规定的十种重大罪名；赦：赦免、饶恕。形容罪大恶极，不能赦免。

例如：（意大利）波施利诺法官和在今年5月23日遇害的法尔科内法官一样，都死于汽车炸弹爆炸事件，同时丧生的还有他的五名保镖。斯卡法罗总统形容这两起爆炸事件是"十恶不赦的犯罪行为"。（《意汽车炸弹爆炸，炸死法官及五保镖》，1992年7月21日《联合早报》第29版）

The Unpardonable Ten Evils

In the penal code of ancient China, ten evils (crimes) were listed as unpardonable. These were the worst crimes.

Example: Like Judge Falcone who was killed on May 23, Italy's Judge Borsellino was killed in a car bomb incident. His five bodyguards were also killed at the same time. The Italian President described these two bombings as heinous and **unpardonable crimes**. (Lianhe Zaobao 21/7/92)

事半功倍　shì bàn gōng bèi

形容费力小而收效大。

例如：要开展泰国的羽球运动，必须先学会泰语，才能指导球员，收到事半功倍的效果。（《语言天才蔡子敏》，1992年5月14日《联合早报》第24版）

"事半"也说成"费（消耗）半"／"力半"／"力省"；也可以倒过来说成"功倍事半"。如果说成"事倍功半"，意思正好相反：费力大而收效小。

To Get Twice The Result with Half The Effort

A switch of the two adjectives in this idiom makes another idiom with the opposite meaning: "To get half the result with twice the effort".

Example: If one wishes to assist in the development of badminton in Thailand, one must learn to speak Thai. Only then can one help to train the players and **get twice the result with half the effort**. (Lianhe Zaobao 14/5/92)

事与愿违　shì yǔ yuàn wéi

事实跟愿望相违背。

例如：许婉仪在参加本届"亚姐"选举时，曾经表示抱有很大希望，因为她喜爱多姿多采的娱乐圈，而且一旦夺得衔头，从此便可平步青云，踏上璀璨（cuǐcàn）星途。不料事与愿违，昨晨竟服药轻生，好梦顿成泡影。（《被取消参赛资港退选亚姐服药轻生》，1992年7月10日《联合早报》第·版）

Things Going Against One's Wishes

What happens turns out to be contrary to what one wishes.

Example: When Xu Wanyi entered this year's Miss Asia Contest, she had high hopes. She liked the glamour in show business and she hoped that by winning the title, she would shoot to stardom quickly and easily. But **things went against her wishes** and with her sweet dreams bursting like bubbles she ended her own life by taking drugs yesterday morning. (Lianhe Zaobao 10/7/92)

拭目以待　shìmù yǐdài

拭目：擦眼睛，表示急着想看到所期望的事物。形容期待着某事件的出现。

例如：影响股市最根本的因素毕竟还是整个经济的走势、资金的流向、个别公司的表现。新航发红股的建议对股市到底能产生怎样的作用，还得拭目以待。（《新航创下另一个"新记录"》，1992年7月27日《联合早报》社论）

Wipe The Eyes To Wait And See

This idiom means to wait and see what happens.

Example: The overall economic trend, the flow of capital and the performance of individual companies are the most fundamental factors affecting the share market. What sort of effect the proposed bonus issue of SIA shares will have on the market we shall have to **wipe the eyes to wait and see**. (Lianhe Zaobao 27/7/92)

恃强凌弱 shì qiáng líng ruò

恃：依仗、凭借；凌：欺侮。依仗强大，欺侮弱小。

例如：我国社会上存在着一些具有流氓心态和恃强凌弱的人，虽然他们还算不得是犯罪分子，但却动辄（dòngzhé，动不动）以拳头恐吓别人，以迫使别人让步，使得我国社会中大部分善良的循规蹈矩者和弱者，在心理上受到威胁，长此下去，人们的安全感自会削弱。（《严惩恶霸，符合社会利益》，1992年7月11日《联合早报》社论。

"凌"也说"欺"。

To Bully The Weak With One's Strength

This idiom means the strong bully the weak.

Example: There are in our society some people who are hooligans and who **bully the weak with their strength**. Although they may not be regarded as criminals, they often threaten others with violence so as to force others to give in to them. In this way, they pose a psychological threat to the great majority of the people in our society who are law-abiding and defenceless. If this is allowed to go on, it will undermine people's sense of security. (Lianhe Zaobao 11/7/92)

数一数二　shǔ yī shǔ èr

不算第一，也算第二，形容非常突出。

例如：吴作栋总理在世界华文书展暨（jì，和）华族文化节和华文报三庆展开幕礼上曾建议，利用新加坡有利的条件和组织经验，把一年一度的世界华文书展办得像亚洲航空展那样，成为世界数一数二的华文书展。（《报业展深受欢迎，将移报业中心再展出》，1992年6月23日《联合早报》第5版）

Counted As Number One Or Two

This idiom, to be counted as number one or number two, means the very best or the most outstanding.

Example: At the opening of the Triple Celebrations (for the World's Chinese Book Exhibition, the Chinese Cultural Festival and the Chinese Newspapers), Prime Minister Goh Chok Tong suggested that Singapore had the advantages and organising experience to turn the World's Chinese Book Exhibition into the World's **number one or number two** Chinese book exhibitions, an event as grand as the Asian Air Show. (Lianhe Zaobao 23/6/92)

束手无策　shùshǒu wú cè

束手：捆住了手；策：办法。像双手被捆住一样，一点办法也没有。形容遇到问题，一点解决的办法也没有。

例如：香港警方前天说，面对越来越猖獗（chāngjué）的偷窃名贵汽车现象，他们简直束手无策，因为被偷的豪华汽车都运过中国边界而消失了。（《港今年上半年1776辆名贵汽车被偷》，1992年7月24日《联合早报》第19版）

"无策"也说"无措"（没有办法处置）／"无计"／"无谋"。

With Hands Tied And Not Knowing What To Do

This idiom means being completely helpless and not knowing what to do in a difficult situation.

Example: The Hongkong police said the day before yesterday that they **had their hands tied and did not know what to do** about the rampant thefts of luxurious cars. This was because the stolen cars were sent to the border with China and simply disappeared there. (Lianhe Zaobao 24/7/92)

四面楚歌　sìmiàn Chǔ gē

楚汉交战时，楚霸王项羽被刘邦层层包围在垓下（Gāixià，地名，在今安徽省灵壁县东南），兵少粮尽。晚上，项羽听到汉军四面都唱起楚国的歌儿来，吃惊地说，汉军把楚国的地方都占领了吗？为什么楚国人这么多呢？比喻四面受到敌人的攻击，处于孤立危急的困境。

例如：四面楚歌的泰国首相苏进达，星期三来到政府大厦的一个房间，准备通过电视发表演讲，不过，当他发现有50名记者在场时，他向记者说了几句便匆匆离去。（《"弄错了"》，1992年5月21日《联合早报》封面版）

Chu's Songs Can Be Heard On All Sides

This proverb means to be besieged by the enemy on all sides; to be beleaguered or to be isolated.

Example: The **beleaguered** Thai Prime Minister Suchinda went into a room in the government building ready to deliver his speech over television on Wednesday. However, when he realised that about fifty journalists were present there, he said a few words to them and left hurriedly. (Lianhe Zaobao 21/5/92)

堂堂正正　　tángtángzhèngzhèng

堂堂：盛大的样子：正正：整齐的样子。原本形容军队的阵容强大整齐。现在多用来形容光明正大。

例如：李资政认为，彭定康须取得调和的首先是行使管理香港内部事务的自主权，接着则须照顾到在1997年后属于中国的利益，尤其是那些中国可以堂堂正正地说是受到香港政府的任何现行政策或决定影响的利益。（《李资政告诉港督，港自主权与中国利益两方面须取得均衡》，1992年7月8日《联合早报》第6版）

In All Honesty And Uprightness

This idiom means honestly and confidently.

Example: Mr Lee Kuan Yew, Senior Minister, is of the view that what Hongkong Govenor Mr Patten must first obtain is the autonomy to manage the internal affairs of Hongkong and then he must look after the interests that belong to China after 1997, especially those interests which China can **in all honesty and uprightness** say are affected by any existing policy or decision of the present Hongkong government. (Lianhe Zaobao 8/7/92)

讨价还价　　tǎo jià huán jià

讨：索取。卖的人要价高，买的人还价低。比喻谈判中或做事前讲条件，要求对方满足。

例如：经过长期讨价还价，日本执政的自民党，终于与国内两个中间派政党，即公明党和民社党达成协议，准备以"自公民"联盟方式在国会通过法案，准许日本派兵出国。（《日本终于要立法派兵海外》，1992年6月3日《联合早报》社论）

也说"要价还价"。

To Bargain Or Haggle Over Prices Or Terms

This means to ask for the best prices or terms in negotiation.

Example: After a long period of **bargaining and haggling**, the ruling Liberal-Democrat Party of Japan eventually reached an agreement with the two moderate political parties in the country, namely the Komeito and the Democrat Socialist Party, and formed an alliance with them to jointly pass a bill in the Diet allowing Japan to send troops overseas. (Lianhe Zaobao 3/6/92)

天方夜谭　tiān fāng yè tán

原指阿拉伯著名的民间故事集，也译作《一千零一夜》，里面讲述许多离奇的故事。形容离奇的不可信的说法。

例如：在没有养狗之前，曾听说过许多关于狗的感人的故事，也看过几部关于狗的忠诚的电影，总觉得那不过是些天方夜谭，是编出来骗人眼泪的；而现在我居然也养狗了。（《我的朋友熊仔》，1992年6月1日《联合早报》副刊《小说》版）

Tales From 'The Arabian Nights'

This expression is originally the Chinese title of 'The Arabian Nights', but is now an idiom that refers to fantasies that cannot be believed in.

Example: Before I kept a pet dog, I had heard many moving stories about dogs and seen a few movies about the faithfulness of dogs. I could not help feeling that those were **tales from 'The Arabian Nights'**, fabricated to cheat tears out of people. Now, to my own surprise, I am also keeping a pet dog. (Lianhe Zaobao 1/6/92)

天伦之乐　　tiānlún zhī lè

天伦：泛指父子、兄弟、夫妻等关糸。家人亲密团聚的乐趣。

例如：八达控股、体育理事会及汽车公会显然已经占去黄思绵的大部分时间，不过他仍设法多争取一些时间跟家人相处。他透露，每年都会全家到国外度两三星期的假期，好好享受一下天伦之乐。（《黄思绵有三忙》，1992年7月25日《联合早报》第17版）

The Joy Of Family Relations

This refers to the happiness of family togetherness.

Example: The Trans Island Bus Services Ltd (TIBS), the Singapore Sports Council and the Automobile Association have apparently taken up most of Ng Ser Miang's time, but he still tries to spend more time with his family. He disclosed that every year he would go on a holiday overseas with his whole family for two or three weeks to really enjoy **the joy of family relations**. (Lianhe Zaobao 25/7/92)

天罗地网　tiān luó dì wǎng

罗，捕鸟的网。天作为罗，地作为网，比喻包围严密：也比喻对敌人、罪犯等的严密防范。

例如：香港警方连同九龙重案组和机动部队，昨天早晨出动一百多人，在流浮山、荃湾及九龙好几个地方布下天罗地网，搜捕前天晚上抢劫旺角瑞兴麻雀馆，爆发大枪战的一帮冷血悍匪。（《传悍匪出现流浮山，港警海陆空大搜索》，1992年5月7日《联合早报》第20版）这个例句用的是上述前一个意思。

Nets Above (In The Sky) And Snares Below (On The Ground)

This idiom describes figuratively the tight encirclement by the enemy or the traps set by the police so that criminals have no way to escape.

Examples: After the mahjong parlour armed robbery last night, in which shooting occurred, the Hongkong Police set **nets above and snares below** at several places to hunt for the cold-blooded robbers. (Lianhe Zaobao 7/5/92)

挺身而出 tǐngshēn ér chū

挺身：挺起身来。表示敢于面对危险的局势或承担责任。现在用这条成语形容勇敢地站出来（担当危险困难的事情）。

例如：香港新任总督彭定康说，他将竭尽所能，为香港人服务，必要时会为香港挺身而出。他说，他会竭力履行 (lǚxíng)中英联合声明，维护港人的利益。（《港督彭定康就职时承诺：愿为香港挺身而出》，1992年7月10日《联合早报》封面版）

To Go Out With A Straightened Body

This idiom means going forward boldly and courageously.

Example: The new Hongkong Governor, Mr Chris Patten, said that he would serve the people of Hongkong to the best of his ability and would **go out with a straightened body** when necessary. He said that he would do his best to implement the Sino-British joint declaration to safeguard the interest of the Hongkong people. (Lianhe Zaobao 10/7/92)

同舟共济　tóng zhōu gòng jì

济：渡水。大家同坐一条船过河。比喻在困难的环境中，同心协力，战胜困难。

例如：吴作栋总理说，我们的社会向来都很重视同舟共济的优良美德。这种互助的精神不只来自家庭、社团，也来自社区。大家只要看看《联合早报》每天的报道，就知道有很多来自不同行业的人，慷慨捐助华社自助会。（《政府决定以一元对一元资助华社自助会》，1992年8月17日《联合早报》封面版）

To Help One Another In The Same Boat

This means that people in the same boat should cooperate when encountering problems while crossing the river. By analogy, it means that those with common interest should work together to overcome their difficulties.

Example: Prime Minister Goh Chok Tong said that our society always valued the virtue of **helping one another in the same boat**. This spirit of mutual help not only came from the families and civic organisations, but also from the community. He said that we only had to look at the Lianhe Zaobao every day to see for ourselves that people from all walks of life donated generously to the Chinese Development Assistance Council (CDAC). (Lianhe Zaobao 17/8/92)

推三阻四　tuī sān zǔ sì

形容用各种借口推托。

例如：中国高层领袖，包括江泽民与万里等人，曾经三番四次邀请日皇访华，但日本政府总是推三阻四，给人的印象是中国急着要日皇赏光，而日本却不很热心，事实却可能并非如此，日皇访华不只是对增进中日关系有利，对日本本身尤其有利。（《日皇到底访不访华？》，1992年7月14日《联合早报》社论。三番四次：sān fān sì cì，成语，屡次；通常说成三番两次/三番五次/屡次三番。）

To Decline Something Three Times And Hinder Something Four Times

This idiom means to find all kinds of excuses to refuse to do something.

Example: Chinese leaders, including Jiang Zemin and Wan Li, have invited the Japanese Emperor several times to visit China. The Japanese government, however, has **declined three times and hindered four times**, giving the impression that it is the Chinese who are eager for the Japanese Emperor to grace them with a visit and that Japan is not enthusiastic about it. The facts may not be really so. The Emperor's visit will not just improve Sino-Japanese ties; it is also in the interest of Japan itself. (Lianhe Zaobao 14/7/92)

拖泥带水 *tuō ní dài shuǐ*

比喻做事拖拖拉拉，不干脆利落或说话写文章不简洁。

例如：李瑞环到底是一个"从群众中来"的中共中央领导人。问他问题，他绝少拖泥带水，连一些本来很"硬"的问题，他都不会左思右想，又或者打一轮官腔，敷衍了事。（《快人快语的李瑞环》，1992年8月22日《联合早报》第2版）这个例句里的"拖泥带水"是形容李瑞环回答问题很干脆。

With Mud And Water

This idiom is used to describe the sloppy or slovenly manner of doing, saying or writing things.

Example: Li Ruihuan is after all a leader of the Central Committee of the Chinese Communist Party who "hailed from the masses". When he is asked questions, he speaks **without mud and water**. Even when hard questions are asked, he does not need cudgel his brains for answers or resort to some official jargon to evade them. (Lianhe Zaobao 22/8/92)

挖空心思　wā kōng xīnsī

形容动脑筋想尽一切办法，含有贬义。

例如：为使毒品顺利过关，毒贩挖空心思所想的夹藏毒品的点子，也使专案人员警觉到，毒贩越来越精了。（《台破获两亿元海洛英》，1992年7月14日《联合早报》第2版）

To Dig Out All Ideas From The Mind

This idiom is similar in meaning to the English idiom, 'to rack one's brains'. It is usually used in the derogatory sense.

Example: To get their drugs through the customs check-point, drug-traffickers **rack their brains**, coming up with all kinds of ideas to hide their drugs. Even then, they fail to escape detection by narcotics officers. So drug-traffickers have to become more and more sophisticated. (Lianhe Zaobao 14/7/92)

万变不离其宗　wàn biàn bù lí qí zōng

万变：变化极多；其：它的；宗：主旨、目的。指不管形
式上怎么变化，本质还是一样。

例如：我们着重的是木偶戏的表演艺术，而不是它的语言
艺术。就算我们用英语演出，万变不离其宗，怎么也离不开闽
南地方戏的风土，戏还是泉州木偶戏。（《泉州木偶来新加坡
讲华语》，1992年6月5日《联合早报》第14版）

To Change In Form But Not In Substance

Literally, this proverb means to change ten thousand times
without deviating from the original nature. The derived meaning is
changing in form but not in substance.

Example: What we emphasise on is the art of performance in
the puppet show and not the art of the language. Even if we use
English for the show, it is only **a change in form but not in
substance**. Whatever it is, it will not deviate from the style of the
local drama of Southern Fujian (Min Nan). It is essentially still the
puppet show of Quanzhou (Chuan Chew) District. (Lianhe Zaobao
5/6/1992)

忘年之交　wàng nián zhī jiāo

忘记年龄的交友，也就是不管年龄和辈分的差异所结交的朋友。

例如：《原野》拍摄完了，马上就被枪毙了，有规定不许这部影片发行。可是，我们成了忘年之交。尽管我们差了许多年纪，尽管我们在艺术上是两辈人，我们还是成了好朋友。（《我拍〈风华绝代〉》，1992年5月30日《联合早报》副刊《小说》版）

也说"忘年之好"、"忘年交好"或"忘年交"。

Friendship That Ignores The Age Gap

This means friendship across the generation gap or friendship between people with a great age difference.

Example: When the film 'Yuan Ye' was completed, there was a ruling not to allow its distribution. In spite of that, we the artistes have become **good friends of different generations**. Our great difference in age does not matter; neither does the fact that we are artistes of two different generations. We are still good friends. (Lianhe Zaobao 30/5/92)

威风凛凛　wēifēng lǐnlǐn

威风：威严的气势；凛凛：严肃，令人敬畏的样子。形容气概威严，使人敬畏。

例如：1984年底，中国的第一家保安公司在深圳成立，人们第一次看到头戴大盖帽、身穿制服的非军非警保安队员，威风凛凛地站在众多企业单位的安全保卫岗位上，或巡行在街头巷尾，维护社会治安。（《中国商业城市出现“守护神”》，1992年7月27日《联合早报》第12版）

Very Powerful And Grand

This idiom means awe-inspiring or majestic and stern-looking.

Example: In 1984 when China's first-ever security company was set up in Shenzhen, people saw for the first time security guards wearing big caps and uniforms. They were neither the military nor the police, but they provided security services to many enterprises and patrolled the streets and alleys, maintaining social order, looking **very powerful and grand**. (Lianhe Zaobao 27/7/92)

为人师表 wéi rén shībiǎo

师表：品德学问上值得学习的榜样。成为别人学习的榜样。

例如：西方人不明白，中国老师的形象并不停留在课堂教书而已，他们强调教师也是学生生活中的老师。黑老师就是这样一个典型，她以老师甚至母亲的身分，照顾和关心马克，马克从她身上学到了为人师表的道理。（《东西文化交流可以通过电影》，1992年5月15日《联合早报》副刊《影艺》版）

A Paragon Of Virtue And High Learning

This expression refers to the teaching profession.

Example: Westerners do not understand that a teacher's role in China is not restricted to the classroom. A teacher must be able to influence his students in their daily lives as well. Teacher Hei is a classic example. From her love and care as a teacher as well as a mother, the students learn the meaning of being **a paragon of virtue and high learning**. (Lianhe Zaobao 15/5/92)

为所欲为 wéi suǒ yù wéi

为：做；欲：想要；所欲为：想要做的。想做什么就做什么（多指坏事，含贬义）。

例如：贾古玛说，如果有一方认为他可以为所欲为，甚至用暴力对付另一方，这种行为是我们不能接受的，我们绝不允许这种事情发生。（《使用暴力者将受严厉对付，贾古玛警告公众不要以身试法》，1992年8月3日《联合早报》封面版）

To Do What One Pleases

This idiom means to do as one pleases, without consideration for others. It is usually used in the derogatory sense, referring to doing bad things.

Example: Professor Jayakumar said that it was unacceptable for one party to **do as it pleased** and to even use violence on another party. We must never allow such things to happen. (Lianhe Zaobao 3/8/92)

无懈可击　wú xiè kě jī

懈：漏洞。没有可以被人攻击或挑剔的漏洞。

例如：当离终点不远时，陈跃玲领先第二名30多米。经验告诉她，这时最要紧的是注意不要犯规。于是她压住步频(pín)，尽量使自己的动作无懈可击。（《陈跃玲飞跃而起》，1992年8月5日《联合早报》第26版）

No Weakness For People To Take Advantage Of

This simply means flawless; with no weakness or fault; cannot be faulted.

Example: When she was not far from the finish, Chen Yueling was leading the second competitor by over 30 metres. Experience told her that the most important thing now was not to break any rules. So she controlled her pace to ensure that she **could not be faulted for anything**. (Lianhe Zaobao 5/8/92)

心花怒放　xīn huā nù fàng

怒放：盛开。心里高兴得像花儿盛开一样。形容高兴极了。

例如：赵剑华在去年泰国公开赛不敌泰国首号球员邱颂蓬；印尼双打四大天王之一的洪忠中与郭宏源，在吉隆坡汤杯赛中输给泰国首号双打选手巴莫与萨卡比；本届汤杯赛，泰国又打进决赛圈。这使教练蔡子敏心花怒放。（《语言天才蔡子敏》，1992年5月14日，《联合早报》第24版）

"怒放"也说"怒发"或"怒开"。

The Flowers In One's Heart Are In Full Bloom

This idiom figuratively describes one who is overwhelmed with joy.

Example: Thailand has eventually won a place in the Thomas Cup Finals last year, with the defeat of Zhao Jianhua last year by the Thai champion Sompol in the Thailand Open Championships and the victory of the Thais over the Indonesians in the Thomas Cup Quarter-final doubles event. Because of all these, Coach Cai Zimin was **overwhelmed with joy**. (Lianhe Zaobao 14/5/92)

兴风作浪　xīng fēng zuò làng

兴、作：起。刮起大风，掀起波浪。比喻制造事端（事故、纠纷），煽动别人捣乱。含贬义。

例如：人们买屋子，通常是供自住，或是为了投资，但是也有人从事投机性的"炒卖"。这样一来就把负担转嫁到真正有需要买屋子的人身上了。较早时，金融管理局就曾向各银行发出指示，希望银行不要贷款给某些兴风作浪的投机者。（《产业市场的过热与投机现象》，1992年7月25日《联合早报》社论）这个例句里的"兴风作浪"是形容投机分子在产业市场不惜采取一切手段，炒卖屋子。

To Stir Up The Winds And Make Waves

To do this is to create trouble or incite others to make trouble. This idiom is usually used in the derogatory sense.

Example: People buy houses either to stay in them themselves or for investment, but there are also those who speculate in properties. These people add on to the burden of people who really need to buy houses for their own use. For this reason, the Monetary Authority of Singapore (MAS) has instructed the banks not to lend money to speculators who **stir up the winds and make waves**. (Lianhe Zaobao 25/7/92)

形形色色　xíngxíngsèsè

形容事物种类很多，各种各样。

例如：我不停地为我的税务官司奔波。在那漫长而复杂的各种交涉之中，我体会到了人间的世态炎凉，看透了形形色色的嘴脸。（《我的朋友熊仔》，1992年6月1日《联合早报》副刊《小说》版。世态炎凉：shì tài yán liáng，成语，形容有的人在别人得势时百般亲热，在别人失势时就十分冷淡。）

Of All Shapes And Colours

This means of many different kinds.

Example: I have been running around incessantly for my court case in connection with taxation. In the long and complicated process of negotiations, I have experienced the vicissitudes of human relations and seen through people **of all shapes and colours**. (Lianhe Zaobao 1/6/92)

休戚相关　xiūqī xiāngguān

休戚：欢乐和忧愁；相关：彼此关连。形容关糸密切，利害一致。

例如：他（菲律宾总统拉莫斯）认为，要扩大本地区的安全与稳定，最有效的途径便是加强区域经济合作。只有这样，才能促使每一个参与的国家认识到与邻国保持友好关糸是和本身的命运休戚相关的。（《拉莫斯在亚细安外长会议开幕礼上强调，亚细安须加强区域安全合作》，1992年7月22日《联合早报》封面版）

To Share Joy And Sorrow

This idiom is used to describe a very close relationship in which common interests are involved. When one party suffers, the other does too. When it prospers, so does the other party.

Example: President Ramos feels that the most effective way to ensure the security and stability of this region is to strengthen regional economic co-operation. Only this will make every country involved realise that maintaining good and friendly relations with its neighbours is essential to its own survival. Each country **shares its joys and sorrows** with the other countries. (Lianhe Zaobao 22/7/92)

炎黄子孙　Yán Huáng zǐsūn

炎黄：炎指炎帝神农氏，黄指黄帝有熊氏，炎黄代表中华民族的祖先。炎黄子孙指中华民族的后代。

例如：尽管大半生的时间都在美国度过，孙小玲还是常常给美国人当成异乡人，因为她的肤色，她的头发、眼睛……都告诉人 —— 她是炎黄子孙。（《东西文化交流可以通过电影》，1992年5月15日《联合早报》副刊《影艺》版）

Descendants Of Yan And Huang

Yan Di (Emperor Yan) and Huang Di (Emperor Huang) were said to be two of the earliest rulers of the ancient Chinese (Han) race. Chinese pride themselves as the descendants of these ancestors, especially Huang Di.

Example: Although she has spent most of her life in the United States, Sun Xiaoling is still often seen as an alien by the Americans. It is because her skin, her hair, and her eyes tell people that she is **a descendant of Yan and Huang**. (Lianhe Zaobao 15/5/92)

掩人耳目 yǎn rén ěr mù

掩：遮盖。遮盖别人的耳朵和眼睛，比喻用假象掩盖事实，来蒙蔽和欺骗别人。例如：美国官员星期二说，当局粉碎了一个庞大的贩毒集团，破获了近七吨可卡因和大麻，逮捕了38人。这个集团利用运输公司和旅游巴士公司掩人耳目。（《美肃毒立大功，破获27亿元毒品》，1992年8月6日《联合早报》封面版）

"掩"也说"遮"。

To Cover The Ears And Eyes Of Others

This means to cover up the facts or to hide the truth from others in order to deceive or hoodwink people.

Example: American officials said on Tuesday that the authority had smashed a large drug syndicate, seized nearly seven tons of cocaine and marijuana and arrested 38 people. The syndicate had made use of transport companies and tour coach companies **to cover the ears and eyes of others**. (Lianhe Zaobao 6/8/92)

夜以继日　yè yǐ jì rì

用晚上接上白天。白天不够用，晚上继续。形容日夜不停地做某一件事。例如：海南岛纬度与夏威夷相仿，最大的不同是夏威夷已开发使用，驰名 (chímíng) 于世，而海南岛仍处未开发状态。许多淘金客群集在海口市，夜以继日忙淘金；海南之美，对他们来说，是既接近，又遥远。（《海南开发十旅游区》，1992年7月10日《联合早报》第18版）

也说"夜以继昼 (zhòu，白天)"、"夜以接日"或"以夜继日"。

The Night Follows The Day

This idiom means to make use of night time to carry on doing what one has been doing in the day, that is, to work on something day and night or round the clock.

Example: Hainan Island and Hawaii are at about the same latitudes. The greatest difference between them is that Hawaii has been developed and has become well-known in the world as a tourist destination but Hainan Island is still undeveloped. Many "gold diggers" - people who want to get rich quick - have flocked to Haikou City, busily digging gold **day and night**. They are so close to the beauty of Hainan, yet they do not have the time to appreciate it. (Lianhe Zaobao 10/7/92)

一刀两断   yī dāo liǎng duàn

比喻坚决地断绝关系。

例如：懂得英文，甚至英文是他们唯一懂得的语言的新加坡人，因为机缘而长住在讲英语的西方社会，以为没有语言的障碍可以使自己在西方社会生活得很自在，事实往往并非如此。他们可以在感情上跟新加坡一刀两断，但是不可能被当地人理解为这是他们前来"投靠"的忠贞表现。（《无认同的痛苦，无痛苦的认同》，1992年7月26日《联合早报》第2版）

Cut Into Two With One Knife

This means to sever a relationship with someone irrevocably; to cut all ties.

Example: Singaporeans who know English, or those who know only English because they live in the English-speaking world for a long time, think that no language barrier can prevent them from leading a comfortable life in a Western society. Very often, this turns out to be untrue. Emotionally, they may **cut all ties** with Singapore, but the people in the western countries will not see this as a sign of loyalty towards the adopted country. (Lianhe Zaobao 26/7/92)

一望无际　yī wàng wú jì

无际：没有边际。一眼望不到边。形容非常辽阔。

例如：黄思绵说，我喜欢大海，主要是在一望无际的海上，能暂时让人忘却一切，好好地松懈一下身心。（《黄思绵有三忙》，1992年7月25日《联合早报》第17版）

One Can See No Bounds

This idiom is used to describe a boundlessly vast area.

Example: Ng Ser Miang said, "I like the sea. This is mainly because while at sea, where **one can see no bounds**, one can forget everything for the time being and really relax and unwind." (Lianhe Zaobao 25/7/92)

一针见血　yī zhēn jiàn xiě

比喻说话或写文章简明扼要，一句简短的话就击中要害。

例如：台湾国家安全局局长宋心濂6月22日在大陆工作委员会委员会议上，强烈批评陆委会对大陆政策缺乏全盘性规划，决策过程也不周全。他并举港、澳政策的规划为例说："目前距九七大限只剩四年，但具体的港澳政策在哪里？"宋心濂这番话，对台湾的重大政策决策过程的批评，可以说是一针见血。（《小动作成不了大事》，1992年7月7日《联合早报》第13版。）

A Single Pin Prick Shows The Blood

This idiom means the same as hitting the nail on the head or being to the point.

Example: At a meeting of the Mainland Working Committee on June 22, the director of Taiwan's National Security Bureau strongly criticised the committee for the lack of comprehensive planning on its mainland policy. Taking the policy planning on Hongkong and Macao as an example, he said, "There are only four years left from 1997, but is there a concrete policy on Hongkong and Macao?"

The director's criticism on Taiwan's decision-making process can be said to be **a single pin prick which shows the blood**. (Lianhe Zaobao 7/7/92)

以儆效尤　yǐ jǐng xiàoyóu

以：用；儆：告诫；效尤：学坏样子。用对一个坏人或一件坏事的处理来警告那些学着做坏事的人。

例如：法庭有责任保护公众人士，那些以为只要付出几千元代价便可以任意打人的路霸，必须受到严惩，以儆效尤。（《严惩恶霸，符合社会利益》，1992年7月11日《联合早报社论》）

Warning Against Following A Bad Example

This idiom means to do something that serves as a warning to wrong-doers or potential wrong-doers.

Example: The court has the responsibility to protect the public. The road bullies who think that they can beat up others and get away with it by paying only the price of a few thousand dollars must be severely punished as **a warning to others who may otherwise be tempted to do the same**. (Lianhe Zaobao 11/7/92)

以身试法　yǐ shēn shì fǎ

以：用；身：自己、本身；试：尝试；法：刑法。指明知犯法，还亲身去做违法的事。

例如：贾古玛说，警方的行动和法庭的判决，已广泛和明确地传达了一个讯息："不要以身试法，否则将面对严厉的处罚；任何人都应该清楚地知道，我们绝不能任由这样的事发生"。（《使用暴力者将受严厉对付，贾古玛警告公众不要以身试法》，1992年8月3日《联合早报》封面版）

To Test The Law With One's Body

This means to defy the law or to take the law into one's own hands.

Example: Professor Jayakumar said that police vigilance and strict rulings had given a very clear signal: Do not **test the law with your own body**; otherwise you will face severe punishment. Everybody should know clearly we can never allow people to defy the law! (Lianhe Zaobao 3/8/92)

用心良苦　yòngxīn liáng kǔ

用心：认真、仔细地思考；良：很。反复思考，很费了一番苦心。

例如：副总理王鼎昌呼吁（人民行动党）党员积极深入民间，听取广大民众的看法，并且协助政府向人民解释用心良苦的政策。（《执政党与人民之间凝聚力比过去薄弱》，1992年7月27日《联合早报》封面版）

To Use The Mind In A Hard Way

This idiom means to give careful thought to a matter.

Example: Deputy Prime Minister Ong Teng Cheong called on (PAP) members to go deep into the grassroots to listen to the people's views and help the government to explain policies which the government had **thought through very carefully**. (Lianhe Zaobao 27/7/92)

有目共睹　　yǒu mù gòng dǔ

睹：看见。人人都看见，形容十分明显。

例如：三年半的时间转眼就过去了，蔡子敏的工作成绩是有目共睹的。

（《语言天才蔡子敏》，1992年5月14日《联合早报》第24版）

也说"有目共见"。

To Be There For All Eyes To See

This idiom means the thing or fact referred to is apparent and obvious to all.

Example: Three years have passed very quickly and Cai Zimin's performance is **there for all eyes to see**. (Lianhe Zaobao 14/5/92)

怨天尤人　*yuàn tiān yóu rén*

怨：埋怨、抱怨；尤：责怪别人。形容遇到不如意的事，就一味地强调客观原因，不能正确地对待。

例如：许多坐过牢的人，总喜欢怨天尤人，埋怨命运。事实上，该埋怨的是自己，因为命运是掌握在自己手里的，过错是自己一手造成的。（《牢门外的阳光希望会温暖》，1992年5月11日《联合早报》第8版）

To Blame God And Other People

This idiom refers to the act of blaming everyone and everything but oneself for any misfortune.

Example: Many prisoners grumble about their fate, **blaming god and other people**. In fact, they have only themselves to blame. One's destiny is in one's own hands. One should take responsibility for one's mistakes. (Lianhe Zaobao 11/5/92)

乍暖还寒 zhà nuǎn hái hán

乍：刚刚开始。天气刚刚转暖，有时还很寒冷。形容季节交替的时候，寒暑变化不定。比喻政治形势或国与国之间的关系不稳定。

例如：近年来的中美关系好像一部正在升降的电梯……从去年下半年开始，这部电梯开始上升，可是美国国内近来要它下降的呼声似乎又大了起来。因此可以这么说，中美关系目前仍然处于乍暖还寒的时期，在明年上半年前不太可能升温。

（《中美关系好像升降机》，1992年7月21日《联合早报》第30版）

Blowing Hot And Cold

This idiom is used to describe the unpredictable temperatures during the change of seasons. Now, it is also used to describe unstable or unpredictable political situations or international relations.

Example: Sino-American relations in recent years are like a moving lift. From the second half of last year, this lift began to move up, but recently there are many people in the U.S. who want to bring the lift down. It can, therefore, be said that the relations between the two countries are in a state of **blowing hot and cold**. They are unlikely to warm up in the first half of next year. (Lianhe Zaobao 21/7/92)

重赏之下，必有勇夫　zhòng shǎng zhī xià, bì yǒu yǒng fū

重赏：优厚的赏赐；勇夫：勇于去做某事的人。指只要有优厚的赏赐，再难的事也会有人去做。

例如：韩国羽总秘书朴（piáo）忠柱在不久前曾透露，只要夺得奥运金牌，韩国球员将能终身获得每月1000美元的奖励。

"重赏之下，必有勇夫"，这真是颠扑不破的真理。（《印尼金牌奖金可能达8万元》，1992年8月6日《联合早报》第27版）

A Handsome Reward Will Draw A Brave Man

This means that a good reward will attract someone to do something even when it is difficult or dangerous.

Example: The secretary of the Korean Badminton Federation disclosed not long ago that if they could win a gold medal in the Olympic Games, Korean players would each get US$1,000 per month for life as a reward.

"A handsome reward will draw a brave man." How true! (Lianhe Zaobao 6/8/92)

忠心耿耿　　zhōngxīn gěnggěng

耿耿：忠诚的样子。形容全心全意，非常忠诚。

例如：自从奥尔担任印第安纳州州长起，玛丽·凯克便忠心耿耿地跟了他八年，协助他料理政务。他出任驻新大使，她也跟了三年。不过，这场宾主关糸将随着大使任满回国而圆满结束。（《美大使饯别会上妙语如珠，捧老婆又赞秘书》，1992年8月21日《联合早报》第12版）

Faithfulness And Loyalty

This refers to complete and undivided loyalty.

Example: From the time when Orr became the governor of Indiana, Mary had been working for him with **complete and undivided loyalty**, helping him in his political affairs for eight years. When Orr became the ambassador to Singapore she worked for him for another three years. This working relationship will end happily with the return of the ambassador on completion of his term of office. (Lianhe Zaobao 21/8/92)

自食其力　　zì shí qí lì

依靠自己的劳动来生活。

例如：阿林目前已经有了一个很好的女朋友。他告诉我，他想做小贩，希望能申请到小贩执照，自食其力，等生活上了轨道后就结婚。（《牢门外的阳光希望会温暖》，1992年5月11日《联合早报》第8版）

To Support Oneself By One's Own Labour

This idiom means to earn one's own living.

Example: Ah Lim had a very good girlfriend. He told me he would like to be a hawker. Hopefully he would get a hawker's licence and would be able to **support himself by his own labour**. He would get married when everything was on the right track. (Lianhe Zaobao 11/5/11)

自投罗网　zì tóu luówǎng

投：走、进入；罗网：捕捉鸟兽鱼类的工具。自己进入网里。比喻自己进入对手预先设下的圈套。

例如：一名"年轻、漂亮的女子"需要钱，130名日本男子自投罗网，纷纷寄钱、寄花献殷勤。这一百多名男子收到"漂亮女子"寄来的充满感情的信后，便寄上鲜花束及现金总值300万日元（约4万9000新元）。但这名"漂亮女子"终于被揭发，原来是一名中年男子。他的公司最近破产。（《"美女"信中诉苦，130男子纷纷寄钱》，1992年7月17日《联合早报》第27版）

Throwing Oneself Into The Net Willingly

This idiom means willingly walking straight into a trap.

Example: A young and pretty girl needed money. One hundred and thirty Japanese men **threw themselves into the net willingly**, sending her money and flowers to gain her favour. After they had received emotional letters from this "pretty young girl", the Japanese men sent more flowers and more cash totalling 300,000 Yuen. This "pretty young girl" turned out to be a middle-aged man whose company had gone bankrupt recently. (Lianhe Zaobao 17/7/92)

八九不离十　bā jiǔ bù lí shí

差不多。形容很接近。

例如：笔者不敢说，周书楷对1970年蒋经国访美这段历史的叙述完全正确，但是，据笔者考察，应八九不离十。（《周书楷谈台湾对美外交的一段往事》，1992年8月12日《联合早报》第15版）

Eight And Nine, Not Far From Ten

This means very close.

Example: The writer would not dare say that what Zhou Shukai had said about Chiang Ching-kuo's visit to the U.S. in 1970 was entirely correct. From the writer's observation, Zhou's account should be in the region of **eight and nine, not far from ten**, very close to what really happened. (Lianhe Zaobao 12/8/92)

病急乱投医　bìng jí luàn tóuyī

病情危急了，到处乱找医生。比喻事情紧急，顾不上选择对像和办法，到处求人帮忙。

例如：被中国选手在本届奥运会跳水比赛中的成功震惊的外国记者们因为找不到中国队的教练，病急乱投医，纷纷向孙淑伟打探中国队获胜的奥秘。孙淑伟的回答很绝："因为我们中国有很好的教练和很好的训练设施。"（《金牌小孩妙语如珠》，1992年8月6日《联合早报》第28版）

"病急"也说"病笃（dú）"，病笃：病势沉重。

A Critical Illness Causes A Desperate Search For Doctors

This means that an emergency will make one look for help anywhere and anyhow.

Example: Foreign journalists, shocked by the success of the Chinese divers in the Olympic Games, behaved as if they had **a critical illness which caused a desperate search for doctors**. Because they could not find the Chinese coach, they turned to Sun Shuwei for the secret of the Chinese victory. Sun Shuwei gave them a fine answer: "It is because we in China have very good coaches and very good facilities for training." (Lianhe Zaobao 6/8/92)

长痛不如短痛　chángtòng bùrú duǎntòng

长痛：生疮时的疼痛；短痛：割疮时的疼痛。比喻与其长期受痛苦，不如忍受短暂的剧痛，求得彻底的解决。

例如：陈天文说，在决定跟琬玲分手之前，我们也不是没有想过要挽回，但感情一旦出现裂痕，修补后还可以维持多久呢？长痛不如短痛啊！（《爱有明天——陈天文准备迎接新感情》，1992年5月19日《联合早报》副刊《影艺》版）

A Long Pain Would Be Worse Than A Short One

The "short pain" refers to the temporary inconvenience or suffering a patient has to endure when a rotten boil is to be cut out, while the "long pain" refers to the enduring suffering he has to experience if nothing is done.

Example: Chen Tianwen said that Wanling and he did think of ways to save the situation before making the final decision to separate. But once there is a crack in a relationship, one cannot help wondering how long the patch-up can last. **A long pain would worse than a short one**! It is less painful to break up the relationship sooner. (Lianhe Zaobao 19/5/92)

大丈夫能屈能伸　dàzhàngfu néng qū néng shēn

大丈夫：有志气有作为的男子；能屈能伸：成语，能弯曲，能伸直，比喻在失意时能暂时忍耐，得意时能大干一番。

例如：华人总爱称道"大丈夫能屈能伸"的精神，汉朝开国大功臣韩信在未出人头地，还在向河边洗衣妇人讨一碗饭吃的时候，曾经受过别人的"胯下之辱"。他这种能够忍受耻辱，奋发图强的性格深受后人的欣赏。（《大丈夫能屈能伸》，1992年6月21日《联合早报》第2版。胯下之辱：kuà xià zhī rǔ，成语，韩信曾被人侮辱，从两腿中间钻过去。形容在不得意的困境下所受的屈辱。）

The Real Man Can Bend And Stretch

This idiom refers to a person who can adapt to changes, showing tolerance and patience during a setback and showing his true prowess when times are favourable.

Example: The Chinese often praise the spirit of **the real man who can bend and stretch**. Han Xin, the meritorious minister who helped to establish the Han Dynasty, begged for food before his great days. He was humiliated by being made to crawl between someone's legs. His ability to bear the humiliation and to strive for betterment came to be celebrated by posterity. (Lianhe Zaobao 21/6/92)

儿孙自有儿孙福，莫为儿孙作牛马

ér sūn zì yǒu ér sūn fú, mò wèi ér sūn zuò niúmǎ

子孙后代有他们自己的打算，长辈不必为他们作牛作马，瞎操心。

例如：中国人有句老话，叫作"儿孙自有儿孙福，莫为儿孙作牛马"。对一般人来说，要为儿孙作牛马，也有他的自由，但是以献身革命为己任的共产党员，如果一朝权在手，就为本身和儿孙谋私利，却是违背人民利益的犯罪行为。（《邓颖超遗言五个"不"字》，1992年7月14日《联合早报》第13版）

也可以单说前一句或后一句。

One's Descendants Have Their Own Good Fortune. Do Not Become Their Oxen And Horses

This means that there is no need for a person to work for his descendents like a beast of burden and worry for them unnecessarily.

Example: The Chinese have an old saying, **"One's descendants have their own good fortune. Do not become their oxen and horses."** People can choose to be their children's oxen and horses. Communists dedicated to the cause of the revolution, however, cannot do that as it is considered a crime against the people to seek to further their own or their children's interest. (Lianhe Zaobao 14/7/92)

好了伤疤忘了疼　hǎo le shāngbā wàng le téng

伤疤：伤口愈合后留下的痕迹。比喻境遇（境况和遭遇）好转了，就忘了过去的艰难或失败的教训。

例如：尽管我们在拍摄中赌咒（dǔzhòu，发誓）拍完这部戏，再也不接新戏了，下一辈子再也不干电影这一行该死的行业了，可是常常是这一部戏还没拍完，就好了伤疤忘了疼，已经在考虑下一部新戏的开拍了。（《谈谈电影》，1992年5月23日《联合早报》副刊《小说漫画》版）"伤疤"也说"疮疤"或"创口"，"疼"也说"痛"或"伤"。

When The Scar Is Healed The Pain Is Forgotten

This idiom means that when the situation has improved, the past hardship or failure is forgotten.

Example: Although we would swear during the filming that we would not undertake new productions and would not take up the damned career in moviedom in the next life, we often **forget the pain when the scar is healed** and begin to consider doing a new movie even before the current one is completed. (Lianhe Zaobao 23/5/92)

女大十八变　nǚ dà shíbā biàn

十八变：指变化多。指少女在发育成长过程中，性情和容貌变化很大，往往会变得更加俊美。

例如：女大十八变，不管有什么目的，打扮得漂漂亮亮的，对别人来说，也不失为赏心悦目的享受。（《大三女生十八变》，1992年8月4日《联合早报》副刊《少男少女》版。赏心悦目：shǎng xīn yuè mù，成语。赏心：心情欢畅；悦目：看了舒服。指看到美好的景物而心情舒畅。）

后边可加一句，说成"女大十八变，越变越好看"。

A Girl Changes Eighteen Times When She Is Growing Up

This common saying refers to the changes in temperament and appearance when a young girl grows up. Such changes usually make her more attractive and prettier.

Example: **A girl changes eighteen times when she is growing up**. A girl who wears make-up often looks pretty and pleasant to others, whatever her motive may be in beautifying herself. (Lianhe Zaobao 4/8/92)

人一走，茶就凉　rén yī zǒu, chá jiù liáng

比喻关糸一般，也比喻事情过去了，情况也改变了。

例如：中国有一句俗语，叫做"人一走，茶就凉。"对一个离任港督，要给予公正的评价实不容易：别了！香江》，1992年7月4日《联合早报》第22版）这个例句用的是第二个比喻义。

也说成"人走茶凉"。

After The Man Has Left, The Tea Becomes Cold

This common saying means that the situation will change with the passing of time.

Example: The Chinese have a common saying, "**After the man has left, the tea becomes cold.**" It is not easy to pass a fair judgement on the departing governor of Hongkong. (Lianhe Zaobao 4/7/92)

杀鸡何须用牛刀　shā jī hé xū yòng niú dāo

杀鸡不需要用杀牛的刀。比喻办小事不必用大的力量。

例如：美国派职业球星的精英参加奥运会，舆论界认为杀鸡何须用牛刀。但美国奥委会却有不得不用牛刀的苦衷。（《美国杀鸡用牛刀》，1992年7月25日《联合早报》第30版）

也说"杀鸡焉用牛刀"，"焉"：yān，哪里。

Why Use A Big Butcher's Knife To Slaughter A Chicken?

This common saying means overdoing things.

Example: The U.S. has sent the cream of the American professional players to take part in the Olympic Games and this has led the public to ask why it is necessary to **use a big butcher's knife to slaughter a chicken**. The U.S. Olympic Council, however, has its own reasons for having to use the big butcher's knife. (Lianhe Zaobao 25/7/92)

跳到黄河洗不清　tiào dào Huánghé xǐbuqīng

比喻受了很大的冤屈，即使尽最大努力也洗刷不清。例如：我（中国著名影星刘晓庆）没有死在"战场"上，却毫毛未损地活着。我恨我为什么没有死，为什么没有受伤，人们会认为我是一个懦夫（nuòfū），我就是跳到黄河也洗不清。（《我在毛泽东时代》，1992年5月7日《联合早报》副刊第7版）

Nothing Can Free Me From Blame Or Prove My Innocence

The literal translation of this proverb is, "Even if you jump into the Yellow River (and use up all the water), you will still be unable to clean yourself up."

Example: I (film star Liu Xiaoqing) did not die in the "battlefield", and am still unscathed. I hate myself for this. Why didn't I die and why was I not wounded? People will think I am a coward. **Even if I jump into the Yellow River, I will be unable to clean myself up**. (Lianhe Zaobao 7/5/92)

一个巴掌拍不响 yī gè bāzhang pāibuxiǎng

比喻矛盾或冲突是由双方引起的，不该由单方面负责。

例如：王薇说，一个巴掌拍不响，摩擦的发生是因为双方都忍不下一口气。一个女人，开车最重要的是注意公路安全，其他少理（《路见不平拔刀相助？》，1992年7月14日《联合早报》副刊《影艺》版）

One Hand Alone Does Not Clap

This common saying means that it takes two to cause an argument or clash.

Example: As Wang Wei said, **one hand alone does not clap**. Friction arises because both sides cannot control their tempers. We expect better behaviour from a lady driver, who should be less aggressive when she is involved in arguments. The most important thing in driving is to pay attention to road safety. The rest can be ignored. (Lianhe Zaobao 14/7/92)

财神爷 cáishényé

中国民间传说，财神爷叫赵公明，也叫赵公元帅。相传向他求财，都能如意。比喻能给人钱财的人，也比喻本身很有钱的人。

例如：如果各国只让日本永远当个财神爷，却不准他在国际政治上有所作为，而它常年累月建设起来的军力又足以让它发威，一旦他被逼得忍无可忍的时候，会不会就此反抗而回头走军国主义的老路，这并非耸人听闻的想法。（《日本应争取各国信任》，1992年6月20日《联合早报》社论。

这个句子里的"财神爷"比喻日本很有钱，也给别国经济援助。

The God Of Wealth

According to Chinese folklore, those who asked the God of Wealth for wealth always had their wish granted. This term now refers to a person who is a generous paymaster or who is very rich.

Example: If countries in the world would only let Japan play the role of **the God of Wealth** forever without allowing her to play some role in international politics, and if her military strength becomes big enough for it to show its prowess, then when Japan is pressed beyond the point of tolerance, will it revert to the old path of militarism? This is by no means impossible. (Lianhe Zaobao 20/6/92)

吃回头草　chì huítóucǎo

比喻重做原先放弃过的事情，或重取原先放弃的东西（多用于否定）。

例如：尽管中国国内现在对经济改革的速度和方式方法存有不同看法和意见，但大家已经达成共识，中国改革开放的航向不可逆转，吃回头草对中国来说没有前途。（《中美关系好像升降机》，1992年7月21日《联合早报》第30版）

To Backtrack And Eat The Grass

This common saying is derived from the adage, "A good horse does not backtrack to graze (literally eat grass)". It is used negatively to mean doing what one has given up or discarded earlier.

Example: Although there are different views and opinions on the pace and manner in which economic reform is carried out in China, a common consensus that has been reached is that the direction of China's reform and open-door policy is irreversible. It is impossible for China **to backtrack and eat the grass**. (Lianhe Zaobao 21/7/92)

传声筒 chuánshēngtǒng

比喻照着人家的话讲，自己没有一点主见的人。

例如：香港民主建港联盟主席曾钰成 (Zēng Yùchéng) 再次否认民建联是中方传声筒的说法。他说，因为鲁平知道他们将与彭定康见面，才托他们传口讯，他们礼貌地接受了。（《鲁平透过港民建联邀彭定康访问北京》，1992年7月25日《联合早报》第20版）

A Mouthpiece

This common saying is used to describe a person who is just a mouthpiece or a parrot of somebody.

Example: Zeng Yucheng, chairman of the Hongkong Democratic Union, denied once again that his organisation was China's **mouthpiece**. He said that because Lu Ping knew that they were going to see Governor Chris Patten, he asked them to convey a message and they agreed to do so only as a matter of courtesy. (Lianhe Zaobao 25/7/92)

打头阵　　*dǎ tóu zhèn*

本来是军事术语，指攻打第一阵。比喻做事冲在前边，或带头干。

例如：46精神党领袖东姑拉沙里，前天在人民力量阵线注册以来举行的第一次会议上被选为主席。会后，他对记者说，人阵将会展开一系列的活动，由人民党在吉隆坡打头阵，然后逐步推展至全国各州。（《主席拉沙里：人阵将展开系列活动，由人民党在隆打头阵》，1992年7月29日《联合早报》第11版）

To Fight In The Vanguard Of An Army

This is a military term which means to spearhead the attack. By analogy, this common saying means to take the lead in doing something.

Example: Tengku Razaleigh, the leader of the Spirit of 46, was elected chairman at the first meeting of the Gagasan Rakyat (People's Might). He said after the meeting that the Gagasan Rakyat would launch a series of activities with Parti Rakyat (People's Party) **to fight in the vanguard** in Kuala Lumpur, and from there it would gradually reach out to other states throughout the country. (Lianhe Zaobao 29/7/92)

代罪羊　　dàizuìyáng

　　古代犹太教每年一次由大祭司把手按在羊的头上，表示全民族的罪过已经由这只羊来承担了，然后把羊赶进旷野里。比喻代替别人受过的人。

　　例如：两名正义力量党曼谷选区议员，昨天写信给众议院议长阿铁博士，指出如果阿铁博士无法劝说执政党与反对党合作修宪的话，就应该辞职。阿铁议长表示，他并不留恋议长职位，他甘愿作"代罪羊"。（《苏进达恫言罢免曼谷市长》，1992年5月14日《联合早报》封面版）

　　也说"替罪羊"。

The Scapegoat

This term came from The Old Testament and is now a Chinese idiomatic expression, meaning someone who takes the blame for others.

Example: Two Bangkok MPs from the Force of Justice Party wrote yesterday to Dr Arthit Urairat, asking him to resign as the Speaker of the House if he failed to persuade the ruling Coalition and the Opposition to co-operate to amend the Constitution. Dr Arthit said he would be willing to give up his position and be **the scapegoat**. (Lianhe Zaobao 14/5/92)

兜圈子　*dōu quānzi*

也说"绕圈子"或"转圈子"。有两个意思：一、比喻走路来回转；二、比喻谈话或办事转弯抹角，不直截了当。

例如："就连北京都不强烈反对日本派遣自卫队，身为日本人为何还要在这问题上兜圈子？"自民党为医治日本人的"恐战症"，在此似乎找到了特效药。（《再谈日本国内如何鼓吹派兵舆论》，1992年7月10日《联合早报》第15版）这个例句用的是第二个意思。

To Go Round In Circles

This common saying has two meanings: literally going around in circles or figuratively, beating about the bush.

Example: "If even Beijing does not strongly oppose Japan's sending out self-defence troops, why should the Japanese themselves still **go round in circles** on this issue?" This statement seems to have an impact on the Japanese. The Liberal Democratic Party, which advocates the sending out of the defence troops, appears to have found the right medicine to cure the Japanese of their war phobia. (Lianhe Zaobao 10/7/92)

放一马　fàng yī mǎ

　　意思是给予宽容或饶恕（ráoshù）。

　　例如：王薇自认胸怀宽大，别人爱怎么超车，爱怎么故意切入她的车道阻挡去路，她都会当对方是透明的，放对方一马。（《路见不平拔刀相助》，1992年7月14日《联合早报》副刊《影艺》版）

　　"马"也说"码。

To Give Up One Horse

This means to accommodate or forgive.

Example: Wang Wei regards herself as a magnanimous person. Whenever others overtake her or cut into her path, she would ignore that kind of behaviour and **give up one horse**. (Lianhe Zaobao 14/7/92)

金饭碗　jīnfànwǎn

　　饭碗：比喻职业。金饭碗比喻待遇优厚的职业。

　　例如：孙小玲终于下决心在80年代初辞去在政府部门的职位，全心全意地投入电影制作。孙小玲的父母都认为，好好的一个金饭碗不要，跑去从事风险那么大的工作，这个女儿简直疯了！（《东西文化交流可以通过电影》，1992年5月15日《联合早报》副刊《影艺》版）

Golden Rice Bowl

This everyday expression refers to a job with excellent pay and conditions.

Example: In the eighties, Sun Xiaoling finally decided to resign from a post in the government and concentrate on film-making. Sun's parents thought she was really mad to give up **a golden rice bowl** and take up a risky career. (Lianhe Zaobao 15/5/92)

开倒车 kāidàochē

比喻违反前进的方向，向后退。

例如：李资政说，开倒车的做法将降低全人类的生活水平。这等于走叫人挨穷受苦的经济学老路。共产主义集团的贫穷和崩溃，已足以提醒人们实行闭关自守政策所必须付出的代价。（《李光耀资政说，东方通过商人开始影响西方》，1992年5月15日《联合早报》封面版。闭关自守：bì guān zì shǒu，成语，闭关：封闭关口。指封闭关口，不跟别国来往。）

To Drive Backwards

This expression means to turn the clock back or to turn back the wheel of history.

Example: SM Lee said that **driving backwards** would lower the living standard of all human societies. It would mean following the outdated economic principles which had brought about poverty and suffering. The poverty and collapse of the communist bloc should remind people the cost one has to pay for a closed-door policy. (Lianhe Zaobao 15/5/92)

卖关子 mài guānzi

原本是说书用语。说长篇故事的说书人，说到关键的地方不再说下去，以吸引听众接听下文。比喻说话、做事在紧要关头有意玩弄手法，使人捉摸不透，借以引起对方的急切要求。

例如：许通美也告诉记者："一个明智的委员会是不会提出一些不能得到大多数新加坡人赞同和支持的建议的。"至于审检会的报告书会不会倾向于采取保守的立场，他表示暂时卖个关子，不肯泄漏半点风声。（《调查显示：我国社会虽然越来越开放，国人道德观念仍保守》，1992年8月4日《联合早报》封面版）

To Sell The Key Point

This refers to the trick employed by the professional story-teller in China. When he comes to an interesting part, he would deliberately stop to keep the audience in suspense. This common saying means to keep people guessing and eager to know something important or interesting.

Example: Tommy Koh also told reporters, "A wise committee would not make recommendations which do not get the endorsement and support of most Singaporeans." As regards the question whether the Censorship Review Committee's report would be inclined towards the conservative stand, he indicated that he would for the time being **sell the key point** without disclosing anything. (Lianhe Zaobao 4/8/92)

敲门砖　qiāoménzhuān

本来是指拿砖敲门，门一敲开，就把砖丢掉。比喻用来求得名利或达到某种目的的初步手段。

例如：如果说中美关系的缓和是由于中国乒乓球队的话，那么海峡两岸的统一，我希望成为敲门砖。

（刘晓庆：《我拍〈风华绝代〉》，1992年5月29日《联合早报》副刊《小说》版）

A Brick To Knock On The Door With

This term originally means to throw away something that has helped one to achieve one's purpose. It has the same meaning as kicking down the ladder after one has reached the top. Now it means a means to achieve a certain initial objective.

Example: Just as ping-pong teams have helped to ease the tense Sino-American relations, I hope I can become **a brick to knock on the door with** that will help to improve the relations between Taiwan and China, and eventually make the unification of both sides of the straits possible. (Lianhe Zaobao 29/5/92)

省油的灯 shěngyóu de dēng

比喻怕事的、好说话的人（多用于否定）。

例如：德国《明镜周刊》的记者麦那访问瓦恩沙，提的问题有点不礼貌，甚至过分。但是瓦恩沙也不是省油的灯，他在回答麦那的问题时说，德波是坐在一条船上，目前民族主义严重，随时有发生战争的危机，如果有百万人逃难过来，我会把他们送交德国。这句话，别说是西方人，连我（作者是华人）听了也会发抖。（《瓦恩沙想做波兰的独裁者？》，1992年5月7日《联合早报》第17版）

也说"省油灯"。

An Oil-saving Lamp

This figurative phrase is used to refer to a person who can be easily tackled without much effort.

Example: A German reporter was very rude when asking questions in the interview, but Mr Walesa was not **an oil-saving lamp**. He said in his reply, "Germany and Poland are now in the same boat. Now nationalism is a very serious problem. In case there is a war, and a million refugees rush across the border, I will hand them back to Germany." Not only the western journalists, but I (the writer), a Chinese, shuddered on hearing this. (Lianhe Zaobao 7/5/92)

铁板一块　tiě bǎn yī kuài

比喻完全一致，没有分歧。

例如：俄罗斯清楚地认识到，西方七国在北方领土问题上并非铁板一块，法德等国出于安全保障上的考虑，还是会在主张积极援助俄罗斯的同时，强烈要求日本在前苏联各共和国核安全问题上作出努力。（《日对俄外交的新课题》，1992年7月13日《联合早报》第13版）

One Single Piece Of Iron Plate

This means completely united, without any differences.

Example: Russia knows clearly that the seven Western countries are not **one single piece of iron plate** on the issue of Japan's northern territory. For security reasons, countries such as France and Germany will still demand that Japan make progress on the issue of nuclear safety with the former Soviet republics while advocating aid for Russia. (Lianhe Zaobao 13/7/92)

钻牛角尖　zuān niújiǎojiān

也说"钻牛角"或"钻牛犄（jī）角"。有两个意思：
一、比喻费力研究不值得研究或无法解决的问题；二、比喻思
想方法固执，纠缠于枝节问题或不值得计较的事情。例如：许
婉仪生前曾透露，"每当感情、工作和朋友问题令我纠缠不清
时，我自自然然会钻牛角尖，钻到解不开死结时，我最想一死
了之。"（《被取消参赛资格，港退选亚姐服药自杀》，1992
年7月10日《联合早报》第16版）。这个例句用的是第二个意
思。

To Dig The Tip Of The Bull's Horn

This common saying has two meanings: the first is to make
unnecessary efforts to study an insignificant or insoluble problem;
the second is to quibble about insignificant details or trivialities and
to get to a dead end.

Example: Xu Wanyi did disclose before her death, "Each time I
am caught in the problems of emotions, work and friends, I would
naturally **dig the tip of the bull's horn** and when I get to a dead
end, suicide would be uppermost in my mind." (Lianhe Zaobao 10/7/
92)